Training Skills for Library Staff

Barbara Allan

Revised and adapted by
Barbara Moran, North American Editor

The Scarecrow Press, Inc.
Lanham, Maryland, and Oxford
2003

SCARECROW PRESS, INC.

Published in the United States of America
by Scarecrow Press, Inc.
A wholly owned subsidary of the Rowman & Littlefield Publishing Group, Inc.
4501 Forbes Boulevard, Suite 200, Lanham, Maryland 20706
www.scarecrowpress.com

PO Box 317
Oxford
OX2 9RU, UK

First published in the U.K. under the title *Training Skills for Information and Library Staff*, by Library
Association Publishing (now Facet Publishing) in 2000.

Facet Publishing is wholly owned by CILIP: the Chartered Institute of Library and Information Professionals.

British Library Cataloguing in Publication Information Available

Library of Congress Cataloging-in-Publication Data Available

Allan, Barbara, 1954–
    Training skills for library staff / Barbara Allan ; Barbara Moran, North American editor.
        p. cm.
    Rev. ed. of: Training skills for information and library staff. 2000.
    Includes bibliographical references and index.
    ISBN 0-8108-4747-7 (alk. paper)
  1. Library employees—In-service training. 2. Information services—User education. 3. Library orientation.
4. Employee training personnel—Training of. 5. Training. I. Moran, Barbara B. II. Allan, Barbara, 1954–
Training skills for information and library staff. III. Title.
Z668.5 .A645 2003
023'.8—dc21   2003009350

∞™ The paper used in this publication meets the minimum requirements
of American National Standard for Information Sciences—Permanence of
Paper for Printed Library Materials, ANSI/NISO Z39.48-1992.
Manufactured in the United States of America.

Contents

9 Training methods 151

10 Running learning groups 182

11 Evaluating training sessions 205

Acknowledgments

Thank you to Dina Lewis for reading this text and providing valuable feedback. Thank you to the Institute for Personnel and Development for permission to use and reproduce Tables 3.2, 6.1, 6.2, 7.1, 9.2, 10.1, 10.2, 11.1 and also several checklists; to the Open University for permission to use and reproduce Tables 3.1 and 4.1 and a checklist; and to Kogan Page for permission to adapt materials for use in this book. These materials are taken from a number of publications, and individual sources are identified on the pages in question. The Institute's address is IPD House, Camp Road, London SW19 4UX. Thank you to the Humberside Training and Enterprise Council for permission to use their version of the learning styles questionnaire. Thank you to other individuals and organizations who have given me access to their training materials. Finally, thank you to Denis and Sarah for providing me with support during this project.

Part 1

Background to training

1

Introduction

INTRODUCTION TO THIS BOOK

The aim of this book is to provide a set of ideas, tools and techniques which may be used by new and experienced information and library services trainers to help them to provide high quality training events. This book brings together ideas, tools and techniques from fields such as accelerated learning, neurolinguistic programming (NLP) and brain research. These have been distilled and presented in terms of their relevance to training events in libraries.

Training events are one way of meeting the training needs of individuals, teams or the whole library. Other approaches to fulfilling training needs include individual learning sessions such as coaching, demonstrations and instruction, and work-based learning methods such as on-the-job training. These alternative approaches are considered in another book (Allan, 1999).

This book presents an overview of the training process. In particular it focuses on the actual delivery of training sessions to groups. The emphasis is on the face-to-face communication process between the trainer and individuals or groups that takes place during the training process. Some aspects of training and development are not covered in any detail in this book and these include:

- the delivery of training via online learning
- work-based learning techniques which are explored in detail in Allan (1999).

This book is not intended to be read as a prescriptive guide to training practice. It presents a wide range of ideas and practices that individual trainers may read and reflect on with a view to utilizing those that are relevant to their own training style and practice. Although this book can be read from cover to cover, it has been written in a style that will also appeal to people who like to dip in and explore specific ideas and approaches. Each chapter contains a brief description of the topic and this is followed by checklists and tables that individual library staff may use to improve their practice. Examples from libraries are contained within the text. These examples come from working documents and practitioners, and they display a variation in format, style and terminology which has been preserved to demonstrate the diversity of different approaches to training within libraries.

The book is organized into three parts covering the themes:

- background to training
- the training process
- professional development for library trainers.

Background to training

What is training and how is it distinguished from staff development? In practice, there is no clear distinction between these two terms as people tend to use the words interchangeably. In this book it is assumed that all training activities have an element of personal development.

Training is often used to refer to learning that is associated with the development of very specific skills and behaviors that are required in the workplace. Training may take place through a wide range of activities including the development of specific skills in the workplace, e.g., through instruction, coaching, and on-the-job training, and also learning by attending specific training events.

Development is a broader term and includes all types of learning that are associated with personal and career development; these may or may not be work-related. Development takes place through gaining a variety of work experience, attendance on education and training programs, e.g., degree in library studies, certificate in management studies, and workplace activities such as mentoring.

The first section considers five main topics:

Chapter 1 Introduction. The rationale for training in libraries
Chapter 2 Training and learning
Chapter 3 The trainer
Chapter 4 Key skills for trainers
Chapter 5 The participants.

Chapter 1 establishes the current context for training in libraries and focuses on a number of themes: the changing context of learning, training and development; changing context of libraries; and preparing the workforce for the future.

Chapter 2 explores new ideas about learning from the perspectives of brain research, accelerated learning and learning style theory. This chapter includes ideas that can be put into practice in any library training activity to enhance multisensory learning. It includes a series of inventories that may be used by trainers and/or their learners to identify their own preferred learning style.

Chapter 3 focuses on the trainer and the following topics: selecting a trainer; role of the trainer; looking after yourself; support for trainers.

Chapter 4 considers training skills covering a wide range of skills starting with action planning and working through to reflection skills. Some readers may find the range of skills required in training overwhelming. However, many of these skills, e.g., listening skills and questioning skills, are skills that library staff use every day, for example with their customers. This section provides additional information and ideas that will enable library staff to develop their skills to a fairly sophisticated level. This will have a positive impact within the day-to-day work of the library as well as in training events.

Chapter 5 looks at the participant and, in particular, focuses on developing inclusive training events for diverse groups of learners. The following topics are covered:

- know your learners
- working with cultural diversity
- working with staff and customers
- working with students
- working with people with special needs.

The training process

The training process may take place at a number of levels within a library: the entire organization, with teams or group(s), with an individual. For example a library may have a comprehensive training and development policy (see example later in this chapter) and this involves all the staff having individual training and development plans. Sometimes training activities are focused on the needs of individual teams or groups, e.g., operating within a particular library or library building. This may be part of the overall strategy or it may arise from particular circumstances such as the opening of a new library. Finally, the training process may be an individual process arising from the motivation of the member of staff and/or their manager.

The training process is a cyclical one and involves four stages as shown in Figure 1.1.

The training process may be the responsibility of an individual training department, a training officer or individual managers or team leaders. In large libraries this process may be the responsibility of a special unit or

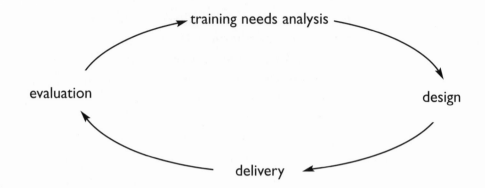

Figure 1.1   *The training process*

team. Typically they may carry out the training needs analysis and evaluation process while the course design and delivery process may be carried out by the same or different trainers. Conversely, in small libraries the process may be carried out by the library manager or an enthusiastic member of staff. However, whether one or five people are involved in the training process then they will need to go through all four stages of the training cycle to ensure that the training provided is:

- relevant to the needs of the organization/unit/individual
- appropriately designed and delivered
- evaluated to ensure continuous improvement.

Chapters 6–11 cover the training cycle. Chapter 6 is concerned with linking training to the needs of the library. It introduces the framework for staff development and training processes within information and library services, i.e., the policy. This is followed by an introduction to training needs analysis and considers the following topics: identifying training needs and identifying learning outcomes.

Chapter 7 covers designing effective training programs by considering two approaches to training design: the 4MAT approach based on Honey and Mumford theories of learning styles (which are covered in Chapter 2); and ten fundamental design principles. Chapter 8 is concerned with preparing the learning environment and focuses on the following topics:

- training administration
- learning environment
- learning resources
- providing a safe environment
- trainer's kit.

Chapter 9 covers training methods and this is organized in alphabetical order (from action planning to syndicates). Readers may want to dip into this chapter to explore or review particular methods.

Chapter 10 is concerned with running learning groups and provides practical guidance and ideas on group processes: from starting groups to ending them and saying good-bye.

The last part of the training cycle, evaluating training, is covered in Chapter 11 where the following topics are explored: evaluation in general, evaluating running training programs, evaluating reactions, learning and impact on the libraries.

Professional development for library trainers

Part 3 consists of a single chapter, 12, and provides a general guide to continuing professional development for training skills, together with ideas and approaches to developing training skills within libraries. In addition it includes two detailed case studies: the EduLib Project and Certificate in Training Practice. Appendix A provides details of learning resources, organizations and also references.

THE CHANGING CONTEXT OF LEARNING, TRAINING AND DEVELOPMENT

Learning: the central issue for the 21st century

Learning is the most powerful, engaging, rewarding and enjoyable aspect of our personal and collective experiences. The ability to learn about learning and become masters of the learning process is the critical issue for the next century.

(Taken from: "Declaration on Learning," 1998.)

This book is written for library staff who are involved in delivering training events either to their colleagues or customers. The library profession has always had a strong tradition of training and development both for staff and, in many contexts, their customers too. There appears to be an increasing demand for library staff to have training, learning and development skills and this has been affected by:

- a new awareness of the central importance of learning in society
- new government initiatives on learning, training and development
- the expansion of the role of library staff into new areas
- new ideas about learning.

In the 1990s there has been a rapid increase in learning and learner development and the idea of developing learning skills has become widespread. Many schools, colleges and universities now run programs to develop learning skills; these are variously named "learning to learn," "effective learner" or "accelerated learning" courses. Variations of these programs are increasingly offered in both public and private sector organizations. The explicit aim of many schools, colleges or universities is to create independent or lifelong learners. These ideas about learning have come from a number of different fields of study such as brain research, accelerated learning and neurolinguistic programming and these are explored in Chapter 2.

THE CHANGING CONTEXT OF LIBRARIES

Ward (1999) identifies a number of drivers which will affect us, our organizations and the information profession in the immediate future. These include:

- intensifying competition
- accelerating change
- continuing information explosion
- communication and information technologies
- information for all
- information and knowledge-based differentiation
- knowledge management.

Both public and private sector information and library services have experienced increased competition in the 1990s and this is likely to continue as we are all seeking to become more competitive. This may take different forms: seeking to increase market share; competing for resources, e.g., within a local government or company, or for research and development grants, or constantly proving relevance and value to different stakeholders in the library. One of the results of this intensifying competition is the increased demand for business and management knowledge and skills in libraries, for example financial skills, entrepreneurial skills, project management skills, project bidding skills, marketing skills.

Accelerated change is a response to increased competitiveness and also to other forces such as communication and information technologies. Accelerated change requires increasingly smart ways of working which are likely to involve both product and process innovation. Library staff are very familiar with increased rates and types of change. Working with and, possibly, moving to the forefront of change require knowledge and skills in managing change, managing yourself (stress management, time management), managing uncertainty, managing multiple projects, and developing learning in organizations and their teams. One response to accelerated change is the development of a learning organization (Allan, 1997).

Ward (1999) states, "The information explosion continues in size, complexity and diversity. Information overload is a recognized stress stimulus and our business is in managing, organizing and enabling the exploitation of information, so that we have control and contain the explosion on behalf of organizations and individuals who need or demand not overload but filtered, validated and authoritative information." The continuing information explosion makes it imperative that library professionals continue to use and develop their information handling skills.

Developments in information and communications technologies have resulted in many new tools, for example the World Wide Web, multimedia, digital photography, advanced information retrieval software, self-service systems. There are also new forms of working and networking within and across organizations and the profession using e-mail, computer conferencing, and discussion groups. Associated with these developments is the requirement for skilled library staff to develop, harvest and support these new opportunities.

Access to information continues to increase and has been fuelled by the Internet. Increasing numbers of people have access to the Internet at home while others get online at work, cyber cafés, bookshops, libraries and educational institutions. It is now possible for many people to gain access to information without ever stepping into a library. This scenario raises many questions such as: What does the library profession have to offer in this changing scenario? How do library staff develop and maintain their IT skills? Who provides basic and advanced information and communication skills within the profession? How are these skills delivered?

Ward (1999) also suggests that "competition and a world of continuous change increase the importance of instantaneous access to significant information. In this context, information itself becomes a key differentiator, for when we all have the access to the same sources then it is our capacity to process and utilize information that makes the competitive difference. Rapid access to information and a culture which believes in the importance of using and sharing information and knowledge are keys to competitive survival." There has been an increase in training events and programs about knowledge management in the 1990s and this is likely to grow as the demand for knowledge management becomes even more important to the survival of organizations and the libraries within them.

These forces for change all have an impact at an organizational level and this varies according to sector but may include some or all of the following:

- changes to structure – downsizing, restructuring, mergers, fragmentation, franchising
- changes to markets – regionalization, globalization
- changes in law – international, regional and national legislative frameworks

- changes in working practices, e.g., telecommuting, computer conferencing, e-commerce
- changes in customers – increased expectations, multicultural, international, increased use of litigation
- changes in stakeholders – increased responsibility, increased outputs.

How will the library profession respond to these continuing demands? Different authors offer different approaches and recurring themes include:

- development of existing library skills
- development of new skills
- development of new and changed roles
- development of new forms of working
- development of new strategic partnerships
- improved marketing of library services and resources.

Whatever the future holds it is clear that library staff will continue to develop their existing knowledge and skills and also expand their skill base to enable them to tackle the new and changing challenges that are presented to libraries.

PREPARING THE WORKFORCE FOR THE FUTURE

The late 1990s produced increased demands on library staff who were often expected to increase their productivity, become multiskilled, to work cooperatively or competitively across different sectors, e.g., public and private, and to work extended days or weeks and, at the same time, live with an increasing threat of losing their current jobs. Different approaches to supporting staff through these turbulent times have developed and these include: training and staff development programs, management and culture change programs, performance management processes, e.g., appraisal and/or progress review plans; management development programs, and coaching or mentoring programs.

Organizations frequently invest large amounts of money and time on training and development for their employees. This investment is required in order to ensure that staff have the appropriate skills for their current and future work. At the same time, there is an increasing challenge to justify the effectiveness of training. No longer is training automatically seen "as a good thing" and increasingly questions are asked such as: Does it provide good value for money? Does it make a difference in the workplace, i.e., lead to increased outputs? Does it lead to competitive advantage? It is the people in an organization who make a difference and the ability to learn faster than your competitors may be the only sustainable advantage.

What happens without training? If a library (or any other department or organization) does not get involved in staff training and development then it may exhibit the following features identified by Whetherly (1994):

- the organization does not meet its objectives
- change is difficult to achieve because staff have got out of or never developed the habit of learning at work
- high staff turnover (particularly of the able and ambitious)
- underdeveloped staff who are not ready for promotion and who feel stuck in the organization and unable to compete for jobs outside
- unmotivated and disillusioned staff.

Lack of training or the provision of poor quality training are not the only reasons for a library or any other type of organization to develop these symptoms – they may also be the result of poor leadership and management (which in themselves are symptoms of a lack of training and development!).

2
Training and learning

INTRODUCTION

This chapter covers the important topic of learning. Apparently 80% of the knowledge about the brain and how it learns has emerged in the past 15 years (Smith, 1998). This new knowledge is only just beginning to make an impact on education and training. This chapter presents a summary of many of the key ideas from this field of study. It covers two main topics: accelerated learning and learning styles.

The field of accelerated learning offers many new (and also old) ideas about different approaches to effective teaching and learning. This section starts with a quick review of some key ideas from brain research. These are important ideas as they tell us how someone responds under pressure and what is required to provide an effective learning environment.

One key idea is that using a multisensory approach, i.e., visual, auditory, kinesthetic (feeling or doing), gustatory and olfactory, helps to accelerate learning. This section concludes with over 15 practical ideas for using multisensory approaches to learning in library training sessions. Although it is unlikely that an individual trainer would be using all of these ideas within a particular training program there is sufficient choice for people to select approaches that they feel competent and confident to use.

The second part of this chapter is on learning styles, i.e., how individuals prefer to learn. Three different approaches to learning styles are covered in detail:

- Honey and Mumford
- multiple intelligences
- neurolinguistic programming (NLP) learning styles.

There is a description of each learning style model and a description of how it may be used within library training situations and this includes specific examples, for example of training plans. In each case there is an inventory which may be used by individual trainers and learners to assess their learning style preferences. With all approaches to learning styles it is important not to use these models to label or stereotype someone. They are best used as an awareness raising tool and guide. Remember that individuals are very flexible and our learning style preferences may change over time and situation.

ACCELERATED LEARNING

Key facts about the brain

Knowing something about the structure and function of the brain is useful to trainers as it provides a rationale and guide for the design and development of training events. The brain is divided into three parts – the reptilian brain, the limbic system and the neocortex; each part has a different function as described below, and is based on the work of Smith (1998).

The reptilian brain

A prime objective of the brain is to help us to survive. When we are threatened the oldest part of the brain (called the reptilian brain) dominates and it prioritizes its survival function and associated behaviors. This results in the following types of response:

- survival – fight or flight responses, lashing out
- monitoring of motor functions – breathing, balance, and instinctual responses
- territoriality – defensiveness about possessions, friendships, personal space
- mating rituals – attention seeking, showing off
- hierarchies – the need to be or be associated with the gang leader, the need to kill other leaders (e.g., the trainer)
- rote behaviors – behaviors which are repetitive, predictable and not constructive.

If learners feel stressed then the reptilian part of their brain takes over. Learning stops and any (or even all) of the above behaviors will start happening. If the trainer is unaware of this process then there can be an unhelpful escalation as shown in Figure 2.1.

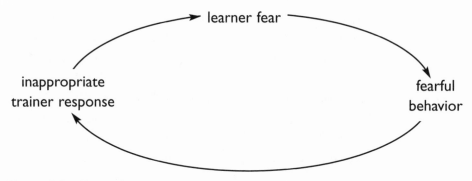

Figure 2.1   *Fear cycle*

CAUSES OF LEARNER STRESS

Stress in a learning situation may be caused by one or more factors and some people are more resilient to stress than others. The following factors frequently cause stress and are likely to have an impact on learning:

- arguments with colleagues, trainer, participants
- low self-esteem, lack of self-belief
- negative self-talk
- inability to connect learning with personal goals or values
- belief that the work is too difficult or that success is unattainable
- restimulation of negative experiences in school/college/university/ other training events
- physical or intellectual difficulties in accessing the learning material
- poor sight or hearing
- learning difficulties, e.g., dyslexia, dysphasia
- distractions in the learning environment.

APPROACHES TO REDUCING LEARNER STRESS

There are a number of different approaches to reducing learner stress and these are presented throughout the book. They include creating a safe environment, providing clear guidance throughout the event, enabling all the participants to become involved with the training program, using positive and encouraging language, using relaxation techniques, and building and maintaining learner self-esteem. A key approach to reducing stress is appropriate humor.

It is important the trainer also manages his or her own levels of stress and remains resourceful throughout the training session. This topic is covered in Chapter 3.

The limbic system

The second part of the brain is called the middle brain or limbic system. This part of the brain filters valuable data in and useless data out (the metaprograms described in Chapter 4 appear to operate here). It also governs values and concepts of truth. The limbic system has a key role in emotions as it controls powerful positive and negative emotions. It is also the site of long-term memory. Powerful learning will take place when it is connected with strong emotions. If there is no emotional link then there will be little learning. One way of ensuring learning is to link it with powerful positive emotions. In practice, this may be achieved by linking learning with individual goals or values. Once this link is made the learning will be valued and then remembered long term.

The neocortex

The cerebrum or neocortex is sometimes called the thinking cap. This is the outermost part of the brain and it looks like a wrinkled walnut. It is divided into two hemispheres: the left brain and the right brain. These are specialized as follows:

Left brain	Right brain
language	pattern
logic	rhythm
formulae	images and pictures
numbers	dimensions
linearity	imagination
details	big picture
analysis	intuition
learning from the part to the whole	learning the whole first and then the parts
procedures	ideas and options
rules	day dreaming and visioning
unrelated factual information	relationships in learning

15+ plus ideas for using multisensory approaches to learning

The following ideas may be used by individual trainers to enhance learning. This is not a prescriptive list and is based on the work of Jensen (1998). It is very important that individual trainers select and use ideas that they personally feel comfortable with and that support the aims of the learning activity.

1 USE MUSIC

Music can enhance the learning environment. It may be used in a number of ways:

- to energize
- to enhance learning
  – to create a sense of relaxed alertness

      – to enhance input of information

      – to enhance long-term memory

- to signal beginning/end of tasks
- to relax.

Music for energy

There are many soundtracks which provide uplifting and upbeat music. Some indicative examples are listed below, but individual trainers may want to use their own favorites:

- "Chariots of Fire" by Vangelis
- "Simply the Best" by Tina Turner
- Themes from *Star Wars*
- "What a Wonderful World" by Louis Armstrong
- "Let's Work Together" by Canned Heat
- "Celebration" by Kool and the Gang
- *Mission Impossible* theme
- *Rocky* theme
- Opera choruses from Verdi, e.g., the "Anvil Chorus" from *Il Trovatore*
- Music by ABBA.

Music for learning

Research has demonstrated that Baroque music helps to create a state of relaxed alertness where the learner is very receptive to storing new information. This occurs because the music helps to coordinate breathing, cardiovascular rhythms and brain wave rhythms. Typically Baroque music has 60–70 beats per minute and this helps to induce what is called an Alpha state in the brain. Some indicative examples are listed below, but individual trainers may want to use their own favorite pieces:

- *The Four Seasons* by Vivaldi
- The *Brandenburg Concertos* by Bach
- The *Water Music* by Handel
- Other Baroque composers include: Corelli, Tartini, Albinoni, Telemann, J. F. Fasch and Pachelbel.

Music to signal the beginning or end of tasks

Music that the author has used in this context include:

- Theme from *Jaws*
- *Mission Impossible* theme
- *Rocky* theme

- Themes from *Star Wars*
- TV theme tunes.

Individual trainers may want to use these or other similar pieces to signal to their participants.

Music for relaxation

There are many commercial tapes available which facilitate relaxation, e.g., collections and anthologies of dolphin and whale sounds, rain forest music, water music, "celestial" music, "angel" music. Remember to be aware of the culture of your group when choosing relaxing music: not everyone appreciates the sounds of whales or dolphins! The following artists produce very relaxing music: Daniel Kobialka, Georgia Kelly, Kitaro, George Winston. Again, individual trainers may want to explore one of these examples or they may have their own favorites to play.

2 USE VISUAL STIMULI – POSTERS, FLOWERS, FLIPCHART SHEETS

Posters can be used to liven up a dull training room. Flowers help to provide visual stimuli too. Some trainers pre-prepare "sayings and mottos" that they display in the training room. Examples of these include:

- If you think you can or you think you can't you're right.
- Every journey starts with a single step.
- Everyone has all the resources they need.
- The meaning of the communication is the response you receive.

Completed flipchart sheets can be displayed around the training room – this helps to anchor the learning.

3 USE SMELLS – FLOWERS, AROMATHERAPY OILS

Fresh flowers brighten up a training room and their smell can improve the atmosphere. Aromatherapy is becoming increasingly popular as a way of influencing the atmosphere. There are now many aromatherapy oils available and these often come with written instructions on how they may be used. Different oils produce different effects: lavender may be used to provide a relaxing environment; rosemary and grapefruit help to provide an uplifting environment.

4 USE VIDEOS OR TV

Video or TV clips may be used in a variety of ways:

- to create a particular atmosphere at the start or end of a program
- as a trigger for discussion
- to put over a particular set of ideas.

5 USE COMPUTER-BASED TRAINING PACKAGES

There are some excellent computer-based training packages which will appeal to many of the learner's senses and are able to provide detailed instruction with self-assessment questionnaires.

6 USE COLORED HANDOUTS

The use of color helps to enhance the attractiveness of handouts and helps to improve retention of information.

7 USE EXERCISES WHICH INVOLVE THE USE OF COLOR

Examples include brainstorming, mind mapping, building collages.

8 USE MOVEMENT

Movement may be used in a number of different ways:

- as a break state
- to raise energy levels
- to enhance brain activity.

A number of simple activities all result in a "break state," i.e., they change the physiology of the participants. Simple examples include: standing up and moving to a different part of the training room, having a five-minute "comfort" break, or a two-minute walk outside.

Movement may also be used to raise energy levels. Examples include: a ten-minute dance to exhilarating music, a quick jog around the building, a game that involves active movement, e.g., a ball game.

Brain Gym involves a series of very specific exercises that may be used to enhance specific types of brain activity. Examples include:

Cross crawl

Cross crawl involves standing and marching on the spot, alternately touching each hand to the opposite knee. Complete 8 to 12 complete movements. This exercise may be carried out to music. It has the effect of activating both brain hemispheres simultaneously and acts as an energizer. It enhances a range of learning skills. It is a useful exercise for trainers to carry out before the course starts.

Lazy eights

Hold one arm straight out in front of you. Point the thumb up to the ceiling. In the air slowly and smoothly trace a figure eight on its side. As you draw the figure eight focus your eyes on your thumb. Keep the neck relaxed and head upright. Let your head move naturally with the motion. Do three lazy eights to the left and then three to the right. Then repeat with the other arm. Then repeat with both hands held together. This exercise increases left and right brain integration and this results in increased balance and coordination. It also enhances peripheral vision (see p. 82). In addition, it helps to enhance comprehension.

There are many more Brain Gym exercises and they are described in detail in the following sources:

Chitty, John, and Muller, Mary Louise, *Energy exercises*, Polarity Press, 1990.

Hannaford, Carla, *Why learning is not all in your head*, Great Ocean Publishers, 1995.

Dennison, P. E., and Dennison, G. E., *Brain Gym: Teacher's edition*, Edu-Kinesthetics, 1994.

9 USE DRAMA

Drama enhances training sessions. Dramatic effects can be achieved through varying our voice, telling dramatic stories, using cliff hangers, and creating anticipation. The use of the Satir technique (pp. 84–5) offers a simple approach to becoming more dramatic.

10 USE STORIES AND METAPHORS

This is described in detail in Chapter 9 (pp. 179–81).

11 USE POETRY

Poetry may be used to catch people's attention and affect the mood of the group. Nonsense poetry may be used to create interest and is particularly useful in promoting creative thinking or problem-solving ability.

12 USE FAMOUS SPEECHES, QUOTATIONS AND SAYINGS

These are excellent ways of starting a presentation. Quotations may be placed on the overhead projector, flipchart paper, card or other presentation media or displayed on the training room walls.

13 USE CARTOONS

Cartoons may be used as an attention grabber, to make a point or to enliven a presentation. Remember that they are covered by copyright and you will need permission to use them. Some off-the-shelf training packages include cartoons that may be used freely. Useful sources of cartoons include:

- Dilbert books
- Charlie Brown books.

Cartoons may also be used as a discussion point.

14 USE TASTE – SWEET OR SOUR

Handing around sweets or asking people to imagine that they are going to eat something like a lemon, will all have an effect on learners. Careful and appropriate use of taste will add another dimension to your training events.

15 USE MIND MAPS, FLOWCHARTS OR OTHER VISUAL TECHNIQUES

Mind maps offer a different way of presenting information and they may also be used for individual or group activities. They are described in detail in Chapter 9 (pp. 168–9). Similarly flowcharts and other visual techniques such as spider charts offer simple methods of presenting complex information. The range of graphic tools available in standard office application packages mean that these charts are relatively easy to produce.

16 USE RAPS, RHYMES, CHANTS AND VERSE

Rap songs, rhymes, chants and verse may all be used to liven up a training session. Music may be played to the group and poems read to them. Alternatively, in some situations it is appropriate to ask a group to write their own rap song or verse. This sometimes happens spontaneously.

17 USE BODY SCULPTURE

Body sculpture is a technique used in many interpersonal skills training courses, e.g., team-building programs. This type of activity is best started by asking everyone to start walking around the training room. The participants are then asked to make a sculpture using their whole body. This may be to represent the team as it is now. This is a very powerful process as, in the team-building example, it immediately becomes clear what the group relationships are. The findings are sensitively processed and then the participants move on to the next activity. It is important to make sure that they have a break state from the sculpture. Body sculpture is a powerful tool and is best used by trainers who have appropriate training and experience in facilitating this process.

EXAMPLE

This example shows how accelerated learning techniques are built into a training plan.

Title: Assertiveness training

Background: This course was designed for library staff working in a public library. A separate course was run for library managers and team leaders. The trainer was a member of library staff.

Aim: To introduce delegates to basic assertiveness techniques.

Objectives: By the end of the session delegates will have:

- clarified the meaning of assertiveness
- identified the differences between assertive and nonassertive behavior
- considered and practiced a range of assertiveness techniques
- developed a personal action plan.

Resources: flipchart and paper, flipchart pens, range of CDs and player.

Time	Activity	Detail
	Learning environment	Music at start. Fresh flowers in room. Refreshments. Positive sayings displayed on the wall.
10:00	**Introduction to the session. Ice breaker**	Ice breaker involves movement.
10:15	**Helpful and unhelpful behaviors**	Brainstorming exercise. Write results on flipchart using colored pens.
10:20	**Types of behavior**	Group exercise involving colorful worksheets.
11:00	**Body language exercise**	Whole group exercise. Everyone moving to different types of music. End on assertive stance.
11:15	**Break**	Refreshments. Relaxing music.
11:30	**Return**	Play "assertive" music as people return to session.
11:32	**Assertive techniques 1**	Description and practice exercises. Exercises involve drama, music and body movement.
12:15	**Assertive walk**	Participants do an assertive walk to rousing music. Trainer coaches them.
12:30	**Lunch**	
1:15	**Brain Gym**	Series of Brain Gym exercises. Some to music.
1:45	**Assertive techniques 2**	Description and practice exercises. Exercises involve drama, music and body movement.
3:15	**Break**	Refreshments. Relaxing music.
3:30	**Question and answer session**	
3:45	**Individual action planning**	Work in pairs. Assertive music in background.
4:00	**Story**	Trainer reads/tells story.
4:10	**Relaxation**	Trainer moves from story to a guided relaxation without a break. Relaxation music in background.
4:25	**Course evaluation**	Using Post-it notes.
4:30	**Course ends**	

EXAMPLE

This example shows how accelerated learning techniques are built into a training plan.

Title: Time management and team work

Background: This course was designed for a team of 16 library staff who worked in a university library. The team included full-time and part-time staff. The trainer was a member of the library staff.

Aim: To enable staff to develop an awareness of their current use of time and to develop strategies for managing themselves more effectively.

Objectives: By the end of the session staff will have:

- clarified how they currently spend their time
- clarified team issues in time management
- explored time management techniques
- developed a team action plan
- developed a personal action plan.

Resources: flipchart and paper, flipchart pens, felt tip pens, range of CDs and player.

Time	Activity	Detail
	Learning environment	Music at start. Fresh flowers in room. Refreshments. Positive sayings displayed on the wall. Examples of time management tools displayed around the room.
10:00	**Introduction to the session. Introductions. What do we want from today?**	Trainer writes responses on the flipchart.
10:15	**Where does time go? Individual diary exercise**	Individual exercise.
10:40	**Where does time go? Team exercise**	Group exercise – involves Lego/Duplo pieces and plastic boxes. Everyone moves around. Music in the background.
11:00	**Process team exercise**	Group discussion.
11:15	**Break**	Refreshments. Relaxing music.
11:30	**Time management techniques**	Description and practice exercises.
12:15	**Time and energy**	Mini presentation. Time and energy graph exercise – drawing on flipchart paper with felt tip pens.
12:30	**Lunch**	
1:15	**Brain Gym**	Series of Brain Gym exercises. Some to music.
1:45	**Time management techniques**	Description and practice exercises.
3:15	**Break**	Refreshments. Relaxing music.
3:30	**Team action planning session**	Exercise completed standing up. Group exercise. Use posters. Develop top five actions for the next six months.
3:45	**Individual action planning session**	Work in pairs. Complete pro forma. Actions must connect to team action plan.
4:00	**Review of time/energy strategies used during the day**	Whole group exercise. Draw day – from a time and energy focus – as a group picture. Trainer processes findings and summarizes with focus on actions.
4:20	**Story**	Trainer reads/tells story.
4:25	**Course evaluation**	Using standard form.
4:30	**Course ends**	

THE IMPORTANCE OF LEARNING STYLES

Individuals all have their own preferred learning style. Effective trainers match the learning styles of *all* their learners. This may sound daunting to new trainers but can be achieved with a little preparation. It results in motivated participants and highly effective sessions.

There are many different approaches to learning styles and, in this chapter, three different models are explored:

- Honey and Mumford
- multiple intelligences
- neurolinguistic programming (NLP) learning styles.

Honey and Mumford provide a framework that looks at how people like to learn while both the Howard Gardner theory of multiple intelligences and the neurolinguistic programming model explore the ways in which someone prefers to take in and process information.

Honey and Mumford Model of Learning Styles

Peter Honey and Alan Mumford found that different people prefer different ways of learning and that most people are unaware of their preferences. Their work (Honey and Mumford, 1992) shows how individual learning styles can be identified. Learning about learning styles gives trainers an insight into the range of learning style preferences in a group of learners.

Their model of the learning cycle is shown in Figure 2.2.

Given a specific learning task, some people will get on with it straightaway, and get through it by trial and error. They are "activists." "Reflectors" prefer to stand back, observe and think things through analytically. "Theorists" prefer to work systematically on a structured program, while "pragmatists" enjoy the practical application of ideas in a common sense way.

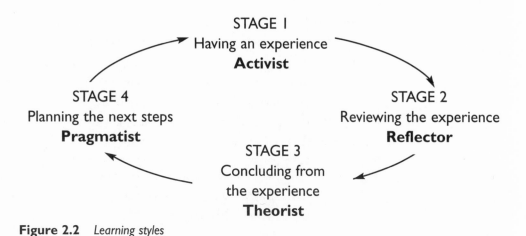

Figure 2.2   *Learning styles*

Though there are obvious drawbacks of typecasting and categorizing people, the identification of a preferred learning style can help trainers to recognize the range of approaches they need to use within a training event. It also provides them with guidance on identifying an individual's preferred learning style and responding to it in a flexible way.

Figure 2.3 briefly summarizes the main characteristics of the different learning styles.

ACTIVISTS

Activists are "here and now" people who are eager to try anything once. They tend to act first and think about the problems afterwards (if at all). They are gregarious people who enjoy being the center of attention. They are excited by anything lively and vibrant but quickly get bored with the routine and mundane. They are creative in their thinking and come up with innovative solutions to problems but lose interest with the implementation or long-term consolidation of plans.

PRAGMATISTS

Pragmatists enjoy new theories and techniques. They can often see instant applications and are eager to try out their ideas in practice. They enjoy the challenge of having a problem to solve and quickly come up with practical solutions. They are rather impatient with long-winded planning and discussion, preferring to "get on with the job." They are tightly focused – concentrating on the job in hand until it is completed. This can sometimes result in tunnel vision. Pragmatists are often task oriented rather than people oriented.

REFLECTORS

Reflectors like time and space to think things through carefully before coming to a conclusion. They listen carefully and gather information to help them make rational and considered judgments. They prefer to act as observers rather than be involved in the thick of things. Because they often adopt a low profile, they may be thought of as quiet or shy. Nevertheless "still waters run deep" and their considered opinions should not be ignored. Reflectors often find it difficult to make decisions.

THEORISTS

Theorists have a methodical and logical approach to most things. They like to analyze ideas in a detached way, asking questions and making mental connections until they have integrated new theories into a comprehensive overview. They are not usually happy with intuitive thinking or subjective judgments. They are often perfectionists with set ways of doing things. Theorists pay attention to detail, which can be of great benefit – or may serve to slow them down and stand in the way of creativity.

Figure 2.3　*Honey and Mumford learning styles* (Described in Fewings, J. (1999). Learning styles questionnaire, *Brainwaves*, Spring/Summer, 9–12, Humberside Training and Enterprise Council)

HOW DO YOU USE LEARNING STYLES IN PRACTICE?

Ideas from Honey and Mumford's theory of learning styles may be used in a number of different ways:

- design of a training event (this is described in detail in Chapter 7)
- as an awareness-raising tool for trainers
- to formulate responses to individual learners
- as an aid to helping learners "learn to learn"
- as a team-building tool.

All trainers will tend to run training sessions according to their learning style preference, for example an activist will tend to include lots of practical activities, possibly spend insufficient time on the theory and leave little time for reflection. This means that there is a danger they will leave some learners behind them. By consciously checking for and including activities and processes that will meet the learning needs of learners whose styles are different from their own they are likely to provide a better training event. As trainers, it is worth while asking the following questions at each stage in the training process: Have I covered each of the four learning preferences? Is one learning style given precedence (and how does this relate to my own)?

Individual learners often let you identify their learning style by their approach to activities and the type of questions they ask. For example, activists will tend to "dive in" to activities and often ask "how" questions. Reflectors like to think about an activity or a new idea before they respond and will often ask the question "what." Theorists often ask the question "why" and will want to make connections between ideas and theories. Finally, pragmatists often ask questions about the practicality of new ideas and theories and will ask "does it work." They often offer pragmatic solutions to group exercises. Once you have identified an individual learner's learning preference then it is easier to match and pace (see pp. 92–4) their learning process, for example give reflectors time to think and not pressurize them by asking for an immediate answer.

This approach to learning styles may also be used to help people assess their own learning style and so become more aware of their strengths and weaknesses. They are then able to develop their weaker areas and capitalize on their strengths. The questionnaire in Figure 2.4 may be used for this purpose. If you do decide to use this questionnaire then it is particularly effective to follow it with an action plan (see pp. 152–4).

Every team will be made up of individuals with their own learning style preferences. By identifying our own and getting to know team members' learning preferences it is possible to celebrate the similarities and differences between people.

EXAMPLE

A team of five information workers in a company completed the Honey and Mumford learning style questionnaire. When they shared their findings they discovered the following results:

Name	Theorists	Reflectors	Activists	Pragmatists
Erze	2	2	6	4
John	3	1	5	4
Simon	6	6	1	2
James	1	1	6	5
Melanie	5	4	2	2

On discussing these findings, the team recognized why Erze, John and James (activists/pragmatists) found it very easy to work together as did Simon and Melanie (theorists/reflectors). They had very similar learning styles. One of the results of their discussion was that the "activists" realized that Simon and Melanie had a very important contribution to make and that it was important to give them time and space to speak – their old tendency had been to rush ahead with activity. Conversely, Simon and Melanie appreciated the contribution the rest of the team made to "making things happen" as their tendency was to discuss, plan and research ideas rather than take action. Using the learning styles model gave this team a common language and new ways of looking at each other and working together.

EXAMPLE

A program that demonstrates the use of learning styles theory as part of the content of the learning process.

Title: Learning styles at work in a college library

Background: This half-day training session was designed for a team of 17 college library, IT and media support staff. It was led by an external facilitator.

Learning objectives

By the end of the session, staff will be able to:

• describe the four different learning styles
• identify their own preferred learning style
• identify the preferred learning styles of individual students
• respond to students according to individual learning styles.

Outline of program

	Activity	Resources	Time
	Music as people arrive. Mozart and/or Verdi.	Music – CDs and player	
1	Introductions – everyone to introduce themselves by saying their name and what they want from the session. Housekeeping arrangements.		15 minutes
2	Very brief introduction to learning styles.	Flipchart paper	5 minutes
3	Activity – why is it important to know and use ideas about learning styles? Small group activity – groups of two to three. Each group to come up with up to five reasons. Debrief. Flipchart findings.	Flipchart paper	10 minutes

4	Learning styles inventory – introduce inventory. Ask everyone to complete inventory. As people finish it then suggest they share their findings with their neighbor.	Inventory Pencils	20 minutes
5	Debrief learning styles inventory exercise. Discuss process. Discuss findings. Give a "health and safety" warning re labeling/stereotyping.		15 minutes
6	Break	Coffee/pastries Music – CDs and player	20 minutes
7	Welcome back. Quick review of four learning styles. Ask people to move into groups according to learning styles, i.e., all activists together, pragmatists, etc. If more than six people with same learning style then split them into two groups. Ask them to identify their likes and dislikes with regard to learning. Ask them to write these on flipchart paper. Ask them to share their findings. Trainer may also include observations re exercise process, e.g., activists are likely to complete it first, theorists are likely to want to discuss in detail.	Flipchart paper Pens	20 minutes
8	Brief input – how individuals ask questions arising from their learning style preference: theorists – why, reflectors – what, activists– how, pragmatists – what if. Discuss relevance to working on a help desk or leading an information skills session.	Flipchart paper and pens	10 minutes
9	Activity – what will you do in practice as a result of these new ideas? Ask them to work in groups of people with different learning styles (try and get one of each in each group). Ask them to develop a list of practical strategies for their work. These need to be written on flipchart paper. Share their findings with the whole group.	Flipchart paper and pens	15 minutes
10	Action planning. Ask everyone to identify one thing that they will do as a result of today's session. Ask them to share it with the whole group.		15 minutes
11	Evaluate the session.	Standard form	5 minutes
12	End the session. Thank the participants.		5 minutes

LEARNING STYLES QUESTIONNAIRE

The following questionnaire is simple to complete (it will take less than 10 minutes) and will help you discover more about the way you learn best.

On the next page you will find 24 questions.

Simply answer each one "YES" or "NO."

Indicate "NO" with a ✗

Indicate "YES" with a ✓

If the answer is "DEFINITELY YES" you can show this with a double-tick ✓✓

If you are uncertain about any answer, count it as NO and put ✗

When you have answered all the questions, complete the score sheet to find out what kind of learner you are. The four main Learning Styles are described alongside the score sheet.

This questionnaire is based on the work of Peter Honey and Alan Mumford. It was designed by John Fewings, Education & Learning (Innovations) Adviser at Humberside Training & Enterprise Council, 1999.

Figure 2.4   *Learning styles questionnaire*

LEARNING STYLES QUESTIONNAIRE

	X	✓	✓✓
1 Do you find it easy to meet new people and make friends?			
2 Are you cautious and thoughtful?			
3 Do you get bored easily?			
4 Are you a practical "hands-on" kind of person?			
5 Do you like to try things out for yourself?			
6 Do friends consider you to be a good listener?			
7 Do you have clear ideas about the best way to do things?			
8 Do you relish being the center of attention?			
9 Are you a bit of a daydreamer?			
10 Do you keep lists of things to do?			
11 Do you like to experiment to find the best way to do things?			
12 Do you prefer to think things out logically?			
13 Do you like to concentrate on one thing at a time?			
14 Do people sometimes think of you as shy and quiet?			
15 Are you a bit of a perfectionist?			
16 Are you usually quite enthusiastic about life?			
17 Would you rather "get on with the job" than talk about it?			
18 Do you often notice things that other people do not?			
19 Do you act first and then think about consequences later?			
20 Do you like to have everything "in its proper place"?			
21 Do you ask lots of questions?			
22 Do you like to think things through before getting involved?			
23 Do you enjoy trying out new things?			
24 Do you like the challenge of having a problem to solve?			

Figure 2.4   *Learning styles questionnaire (continued)*

	P	A	R	T
1				
2				
3				
4				
5				
6				
7				
8				
9				
10				
11				
12				
13				
14				
15				
16				
17				
18				
19				
20				
21				
22				
23				
24				
Totals				

HOW TO SCORE

For each statement write your score in the <u>unshaded</u> box. *Ticks* count as <u>1 point</u>. *Double-ticks* count as <u>2 points</u>. *Crosses* count as <u>0.</u> Count up the number of points in each column and write the totals at the bottom. This gives you a score for each of the four Learning Styles explained below. Although most people exhibit a mixture of styles, it is often apparent that they have a dominant style. Understanding yours can help you to become a more effective learner.

PRAGMATISTS

Pragmatists enjoy new theories and techniques. They can often see instant applications and are keen to try out their ideas in practice. They enjoy the challenge of having a problem to solve and quickly come up with practical solutions. They are rather impatient with long-winded planning and discussion, preferring to "get on with the job." They are tightly focused – concentrating on the job in hand until it is completed. This can sometimes result in tunnel vision. Pragmatists are often task oriented rather than people oriented.

ACTIVISTS

Activists are "here and now" people who are keen to try anything once. They tend to act first and think about the problems afterwards (if at all). They are gregarious people who enjoy being the center of attention. They are excited by anything lively and vibrant but quickly get bored with the routine and mundane. They are creative in their thinking and come up with innovative solutions to problems but lose interest with the implementation or long-term consolidation of plans.

REFLECTORS

Reflectors like time and space to think things through carefully before coming to a conclusion. They listen carefully and gather information to help them make rational and considered judgments. They prefer to act as observers rather than be involved in the thick of things. Because they often adopt a low profile, they may be thought of as quiet or shy. Nevertheless "still waters run deep" and their considered opinions should not be ignored. Reflectors often find it difficult to make decisions.

THEORISTS

Theorists have a methodical and logical approach to most things. They like to analyze ideas in a detached way, asking questions and making mental connections until they have integrated new theories into a comprehensive overview. They are not usually happy with intuitive thinking or subjective judgments. They are often perfectionists with set ways of doing things. Theorists pay attention to detail, which can be of great benefit – or may serve to slow them down and stand in the way of creativity.

WHICH IS THE "BEST" LEARNING STYLE?

No one of the four Learning Styles can be said to be any better than any of the others. In certain circumstances, one or the other of the styles will be better suited to the task in hand or to the teaching methods being used. They each have their strong points – and they each have their drawbacks. What is important is that you discover your own style – so that you can play to your strengths – and do something to overcome or compensate for those drawbacks. We hope that completing this questionnaire has helped you to think about the way you like to learn.

Figure 2.4   *Learning styles questionnaire* (continued)

Multiple intelligences

Howard Gardner, a psychologist based at Harvard University, suggests that the traditional concept of intelligence is too narrow and doesn't take into account the wider range of preferred learning styles which are demonstrated by different people. He identifies a wide range of preferred learning styles and, in this section, we are going to concentrate on eight of them.

Gardner suggests that the following learning styles represent the vast majority of learners:

- linguistic – involves use of words and language, enjoyment of books, dialog and jokes
- mathematical/logical – involves step-by-step processes, looking for patterns, rational and well ordered
- musical – involves music, rhythm, pitch, tone and pattern
- visual/spatial – involves looking at things and seeing the whole picture as well as the details, ability to read maps, diagrams and charts, ability to understand where things are in relationship to each other
- interpersonal – involves working with others, understanding other people's emotions and motivations
- intrapersonal – involves going into yourself and perhaps daydreaming, thinking things through in your head
- emotional – involves understanding ourselves and our emotions
- bodily/physical – involves physical activities and all other kinds of activities.

Howard Gardner suggests that traditional forms of learning and education are chiefly based on using linguistic and mathematical/logical learning styles. Apparently, only 15% of the population have this learning profile which suggests that for the remaining 85% a different approach to learning is required if they are to achieve their potential. He suggests that a trainer needs to take into account this wide range of approaches to meet everyone's learning needs and to help learners achieve their potential.

How do you use the model in practice?

The ideas of Howard Gardner may be used in a number of different ways:

- to help learners identify and develop their learning to learn skills
- to help trainers identify their training strengths and potential weaknesses
- as an aid to preparing training sessions.

Individual learners may be introduced to these ideas and helped to identify their own preferred intelligences. This is easily achieved using the type of questionnaire presented in Figure 2.5.

Linguistic

I enjoy puns and jokes ❑

I enjoy listening to others ❑

I enjoy poetry and plays ❑

I enjoy learning from books, tapes, discussions and lectures ❑

I enjoy writing ❑

I frequently contact people for new information or to discuss matters ❑

Mathematical/logical

I enjoy numbers ❑

I enjoy puzzles and riddles ❑

I like logical "step-by-step" explanations ❑

I enjoy chess and similar games ❑

I like to work through problems in a logical way ❑

I enjoy breaking codes ❑

Visual/spatial

I like to learn by looking at charts, diagrams and pictures ❑

I enjoy watching videos and films ❑

I am good at picturing things in my mind ❑

In sports, I often "know" where the ball is going to land next ❑

I find it easy to park my car in a small space ❑

I enjoy drawing and painting ❑

Musical

I like to listen to and/or make music ❑

I notice sounds when I am working ❑

I find that I can easily be distracted by sound or music ❑

I have a good sense of rhythm ❑

I find it easy to learn and remember the words of songs ❑

I am constantly humming, tapping and singing ❑

Interpersonal

I enjoy working with other people ❑

I am interested in the relationships that exist between other people ❑

I like spending my spare time with other people ❑

I don't enjoy working by myself ❑

I am able to help sort out conflict between other people ❑

I can quickly establish myself in a new group ❑

Emotional

I am sensitive to the feelings of others ❑

I understand my own feelings ❑

I am able to let people know how I feel ❑

Figure 2.5 *Multiple intelligences questionnaire* (Adapted from K. Burden et al., *Learning to learn: teacher's pack,* Center for Learning, 1995)

I am able to manage my feelings if I feel upset or under stress ❏

I understand what triggers negative feelings in me ❏

I find it easy to empathize with others ❏

Intrapersonal

I enjoy daydreaming ❏

I frequently make up stories in my head ❏

I like to work by myself ❏

I like peace and quiet ❏

I think about what I do and how I do things ❏

I enjoy writing a diary or imaginative stories ❏

Bodily/physical

I enjoy physical exercise ❏

I like to be actively involved in doing things ❏

I remember things best when I have done something (rather than seen or heard something) ❏

I don't like sitting still for a long period of time ❏

I like to touch and play with things ❏

I like to work with objects that feel good ❏

Figure 2.5 *Multiple intelligences questionnaire (continued)*

It is useful for individual trainers to identify their own preferred intelligences. This is because individual trainers are likely to use their preferred styles in their training programs and may not use their weaker styles. This is likely to disadvantage some learners. By identifying our preferred intelligences it is then possible to ensure that we develop our weaker styles and also provide learning opportunities in all styles in our training programs. Again, the questionnaire in Figure 2.5 may be used by individual trainers to identify their learning preferences.

The idea of multiple intelligences can be used in the design of a training program. Training sessions which cater to all the different learning styles are likely to be more interesting and relevant to all of the learners. They are likely to engage more of the whole brain activity and enhance the quality of learning. As a trainer have you covered all the different intelligences in your training plan? The worksheet in Figure 2.6 may be copied and used as an aid to planning training sessions.

Time	Activity	Linguistic	Mathematical/ logical	Visual/ spatial	Musical	Interpersonal	Emotional	Intrapersonal	Bodily/ physical

Figure 2.6 *Planning learning sessions using Howard Gardner's model of multiple intelligences*

EXAMPLE

This example program was designed by a secondary school librarian.

Title: Learning to win

Background: Used by a school librarian in a study skills session. The session is 60 minutes long. This session has been designed for a group of 24 6th grade pupils (aged 11 years).

Aim: The aim of this session is to improve pupil learning by the use of multiple intelligences.

Objectives: By the end of the session, pupils will be able to:

*   list the eight main learning styles
*   know their preferred learning style(s)
*   identify one way in which they will use this information next week.

Notes: Resources needed: handout showing the different multiple intelligences, questionnaire, calendars.

Program

1 Welcome. Introduction to multiple intelligences. (5 minutes)
2 Why knowledge of multiple intelligences can help them do better at school. (5 minutes)
3 What are the different intelligences – explanation and handout. (10 minutes)
4 What are your preferred learning styles – questionnaire. (10 minutes)
5 How do I like to learn – pairs activity (partner with same/similar preferences). (10 minutes)
6 Different ways of using this information – class discussion. Ideas written up on whiteboard. (10 minutes)
7 Individual action planning – write in calendar – one way in which I will use these ideas in the following week. (8 minutes)
8 Finish off. End session. (2 minutes)

EXAMPLE

Sample program designed by two children's librarians.

Title: Circus fun

Background: Used as a public library activity session for readers aged between 6 and 9. This program was led by two children's librarians.

Aim: The aim of this session is to encourage children to read more books.

Objectives: By the end of the session, children will have:

- played with circus equipment
- completed a book quiz
- heard two stories and two poems
- watched a video clip
- made a mask
- seen a magician's act.

Notes: Resources needed: quiz, two circus stories and two/three circus poems, clown (!), circus equipment (juggling balls, etc.), magician (!), current video clip, mask making equipment, badges and prizes.

Program

Time	Activity	Linguistic	Mathematical/ logical	Visual/ spatial	Musical	Inter- personal	Emotional	Intra- personal	Bodily/ physical
10:00	Welcome. Staff dressed as as clowns welcome and introduce everyone. Give out name badges.	•		•		•			
10:05	Hand out juggling and other apparatus. Four set games – children in pairs. Circus music in background.			•	•				•
10:25	Read from circus story 1.	•					•	•	
10:40	Quiz – Ten questions, answers in reference books. Work in teams of three.	•	•	•		•			•
11:00	Read from circus story 2.	•					•	•	
11:05	Mask making activity. Video clip on in background.			•	•	•	•		•
11:25	Wear masks and watch magician.	•		•			•	•	
11:55	Three poems.	•					•	•	
12:00	End								

Neurolinguistic programming learning styles

Bandler and Grinder developed a model of communication based on very detailed observation of expert communicators and their model is known as neurolinguistic programming (NLP). NLP looks at how people prefer to organize and access information in their mind. They have found that individuals tend to prefer one of three main methods, or sensory modes, of taking in and learning information. The main styles are:

- visual
- auditory
- kinesthetic.

Visual people prefer to take in new information in a visual form, e.g., pictures, charts or diagrams, and like to visualize information. Auditory people may prefer to listen and talk through new ideas. They frequently remember the tone and exact content of different conversations. In contrast, kinesthetic learners like to be actively involved in doing things and like to touch and handle things. According to Smith (1998) the following breakdown shows how these different learning styles are represented:

- visual learners 29%
- auditory learners 34%
- kinesthetic learners 37%.

It is relatively simple to identify the preferred NLP learning style of an individual learner. The language they use will give clues to their preferred thinking and learning style. Figure 2.7 outlines typical language patterns that someone will use. If we match a learner's preferred style, for example through the teaching and training methods we use, and also by the language we use, they are more likely to understand and remember the new ideas. In a group, there will be learners with each of the three VAK learning styles. The most effective trainers are those who express ideas in different ways to cover all three preferences, so that all the learners will have access to the ideas.

Visual learners will use and respond to phrases like:

I see that now	That looks right
Let's get this into perspective	I'm in the dark on this one
I get the picture	I can't see where we are going
It appears to me	What's your view

and they will use terms such as:

picture, focus, image, clear, reflect, clarify, visualize, see, notice, illustrate, show, perspective, view, vision.

Auditory learners will use and respond to phrases such as:

That rings a bell	I don't like the sound of that
I get the message loud and clear	That strikes a chord
I can't hear what I'm thinking	That's music to my ears
I've got the message	

and they will use terms such as:

audible, remark, sound, harmonious, accent, rhythm, discuss, listen, tone, ask, hear, speechless, quiet, shout.

Kinesthetic learners frequently use phrases such as:

How does that grab you?

It doesn't feel right to me

Give me a concrete example

He is a slippery customer

She has a firm grasp of the subject

and they will use terms such as:

touch, feel, push, handle, move, fix, mend, stress, sensitive, tension, grasp, hold, warm, cold, rough, smooth, touchy, pushover, contact, sort out.

Figure 2.7 *Language and learning styles*

This model is compatible with Gardner's model (see pp. 31–5) as it offers a detailed analysis of three of Gardner's eight learning styles, i.e., visual/spatial, musical and bodily/physical. It is useful to be aware of both models and individual trainers may wish to apply one or both models in their own learning situations.

HOW DO YOU USE IT IN PRACTICE?

These ideas from the field of neurolinguistic programming may be used in exactly the same way as the Honey and Mumford model of learning styles and Howard Gardner's theory of multiple intelligences, that is:

- to help learners identify and develop their learning to learn skills
- to help trainers identify the learning styles of others and then match these styles

- to help trainers identify their training strengths and potential weaknesses
- as an aid to preparing training sessions.

A questionnaire for assisting individual learners and trainers to identify their own learning styles is presented in Figure 2.8. As with other approaches to learning styles it is important not to use this to label or stereotype someone. Use it as an awareness raising tool and guide and

---

HOW DO YOU LIKE TO PRESENT NEW IDEAS?

Check the boxes to indicate which activities you normally use as part of your teaching/training practice. Add up your scores and identify your preferred style.

Visual Methods

Make diagrams or use mind maps ☐

Show a video ☐

Give a demonstration ☐

Use maps, charts, diagrams ☐

Use an OHP ☐

Ask learners to visualize something ☐

TOTAL NUMBER OF CHECKS ___

Auditory Methods

Use tapes/CD-ROMs with music ☐

Explain something ☐

Use radio ☐

Provide opportunities for learners to talk ☐

Read materials out aloud ☐

Ask learners to explain ideas to another learner ☐

TOTAL NUMBER OF CHECKS ___

Kinesthetic Methods

Create opportunities for learners to move ☐

Use role play, competitions, drama, simulations ☐

Ask learners to do something as they learn, e.g., writing,

doodling, underlining, selecting items ☐

Use practical exercises, e.g., workbooks ☐

Use experiments ☐

Offer opportunities for creativity, e.g., making up activities,

presentations ☐

TOTAL NUMBER OF CHECKS ___

Figure 2.8   *Learning styles questionnaire for trainers* (Adapted from K. Burden et al., *Learning to learn: teacher's pack,* Centre for Learning, 1995)

remember that individuals are very flexible and our learning style preferences may change over time and situation.

A form for preparing training sessions so that they cover all the different learning styles is presented in Figure 2.9. You may like to use this to help you design or assess your own training sessions.

Use this worksheet as a form for planning your training sessions. Complete the sheet identifying the different activities which will be included in your training event. Then check whether or not you are covering visual, auditory and kinesthetic learning styles.

Time	Activity	Visual	Auditory	Kinesthetic

Figure 2.9   *Planning learning sessions using Bandler and Grinder's Model*

EXAMPLE

This program was designed by an external trainer.

Title: Team building for the future

Background: This event was designed and led by an external trainer. It was provided for a group of eight information staff working in a legal services organization.

Aims: The aim of this event is to improve teamwork within the library team.

Learning objectives: By the end of the event, team members will have:

*   identified the characteristics of an excellent team
*   assessed their own team strengths and areas of development
*   explored a model for effective teamwork
*   developed a team action plan
*   developed individual action plans.

Resources: flowers; flipchart, paper and pens; teamwork inventory; range of CDs and player.

Time	Activity	Visual	Auditory	Kinesthetic
	Prepare room. Welcome sign – flipchart. Flowers. Music. Coffee/tea on arrival.	V	A	K
9:15	Introductions. Housekeeping.	V	A	
9:30	General introduction to the course. Objectives. Participants work in pairs. What I want to get out of the day (5 minutes). Flipchart findings.	V	A	K
9:45	Characteristics of an effective team. Brainstorm. Write on flipchart.	V	A	
10:00	Introduction to teamwork theory and framework. Team building activity. Music in background.	V	A	K
11:00	Break with refreshments. Put on music.	V	A	
11:15	Debrief activity.	V	A	K
12:00	Teamwork inventory. Complete questionnaire. Music.	V	A	K
12:30	Discussion. Any questions. End morning session.	V	A	
12:30–1:15	Lunch	V	A	K
1:15	Video on teamwork. Participants complete questionnaire using information from video. Hand out mints. Discussion.	V	A	K
2:15	Implications for team leaders. Discussion. Flipchart key points.	V	A	
2:45	Implications for team members. Pairs exercise. Use worksheet.	V	A	K
3:15	Break with refreshments. Put on music.	V	A	K
3:30	Team action planning session – group exercise carried out standing up. Flipchart top ten actions.	V	A	K
4:00	Individual action planning – pairs exercise.	V	A	
4:20	Course evaluation.	V		
4:30	End	V	A	

3
The trainer

INTRODUCTION

This chapter is concerned with library staff as trainers and it explores four important topics:

- selecting a trainer
- role of the trainer
- looking after yourself
- support for trainers.

The first section is concerned with choosing a trainer and looks at the advantages and disadvantages of using an in-house or external trainer. This is followed by a section that looks at the role of the library trainer. Library trainers are involved in a number of different roles depending on their level of involvement in the different stages of the training cycle. In addition, when they are delivering learning or training programs they may step into a variety of roles from teacher to counsellor. The skills trainers need are covered in detail in Chapter 4.

The third section of this chapter is concerned with "looking after yourself." Working in a busy library environment many staff are asked to add running training events to their already busy schedules. Unless they look after themselves and prepare for the physical, mental and emotional challenge of training then they are unlikely to provide a high quality training session. The topics covered in this section include health and fitness, resourceful states and energy. The energy section includes seven energy-raising strategies.

The final section is concerned with finding and using personal support. This may be during the training event, for example through cotraining or the support of voluntary training assistants, or outside the training arena with a mentor who is able to provide guidance and support for your specific work as a trainer. It is very common practice for library staff to have a work-based mentor and it is possible that this person may also be able to offer support for training activities. If not, then it is worthwhile exploring the possibility of additional mentoring support for the training activity.

SELECTING A TRAINER

A wide range of people are involved in the delivery of staff development within information and library services and they include staff who are internal to the library and external trainers. There are a number of different advantages and disadvantages to using in-house or external trainers outlined in Table 3.1.

In-house trainers may be staff development officers or organizational staff development and training officers. If you are considering using an

Table 3.1 *Advantages and disadvantages of in-house or external trainers* (Adapted from Open University, *Planning, monitoring and evaluating learning programs,* People and Potential, Study Unit 3, 1994)

	Advantages	**Disadvantages**
In-house trainer	Understand library, its aims, objectives and culture	May lack training and development skills
	Know the library, its systems and procedures	Can be out-of-date or only familiar with a narrow range of knowledge/skills
	Know individuals and their learning styles	Their position in the organization may mean that they lack credibility or participants will not trust them
	Relatively cheap (costs hidden in other that budgets)	Their history within the library may mean they have "baggage" or their colleagues have "baggage" about the trainer
		They may have insufficient time to carry out sufficient research and preparation for the event
		They may be cynical about the library, its managers and the training program
External trainer	Can bring a fresh approach and new ideas	If they have not been well briefed then they will not meet the objectives of your event
	They are free from being part of the internal situation and historical "baggage"	They may question organizational policy inappropriately
	They tend to specialize in particular areas so their knowledge and skills should be up-to-date	They can raise expectations of learners that cannot be met back in the workplace
	They can support in-house programs and help to bring even more credibility to in-house trainers	If the library is not actively involved then it may lose control of the learner's development
	They can offer benchmarking with other organizations	Course follow-up and support mechanisms may not take place
		They tend to be more expensive than in-house trainers

internal trainer then Hackett (1997) suggests that you need to consider the following factors:

- subject expertise
- training skills
- commitment to helping others learn
- competence in using relevant training methods
- credibility with participants
- availability.

Sometimes sensitive decisions need to be made, for example a senior manager may assume that they will be asked to run a training session and from experience you know that:

- they won't prepare the session properly
- they will use badly prepared training materials
- they will make inappropriate comments about the library.

This situation does arise and needs to be handled appropriately.

External trainers may be staff from other information and library organization, staff from other organizations (including professional associations) or independent trainers. If you are seeking an external trainer then it is worthwhile identifying your selection criteria and these may include:

- ability to meet your training needs and specific learning outcomes
- reputation – of the trainer's organization and the individual(s)
- match with own library culture and ethos
- availability
- cost
- geographic location.

Hackett's (1997) description of the process for selecting external providers is given in Table 3.2.

THE ROLE OF THE TRAINER

Trainers take on a number of different roles and this will be in addition to their other library roles. In terms of the overall training process or cycle every trainer is likely to undertake some of the following activities and a few trainers may undertake all of them:

- training needs analysis
- planning of training events
- design of training events
- development of supporting learning resources

Table 3.2 *Selecting external providers* (Adapted from P. Hackett, *Introduction to training,* IPD, 1997)

	Process	Explanation
1	**Research the options**	This could involve phoning colleagues in other libraries, making enquiries at conferences and other networking events, contacting professional associations, reading the professional literature.
2	**Consider the wider issues**	If the proposed training is the first step in a larger training plan it may make sense to start with someone who will be able to contribute more later – reducing the amount of familiarization time that will be needed before subsequent stages. Against this must be weighed the issue of trainer credibility. While familiarity will save time, having the same so-called "specialist" popping up on six different subjects may stretch their credibility in the eyes of trainees.
3	**Clarify the detail**	What is the provider offering to do? When, where and for how many trainees? Over how long a period and at what cost? What learning methods will they use? What are the guarantees of success?
4	**Impartially weigh up the pros and cons of each option**	Apply your selection criteria as objectively as possible. It is always worthwhile seeing a prospective trainer in action before you make the final decision. Check with other information and library organizations which have used this supplier.
5	**Make a decision or recommend an appropriate provider**	If you are the decision maker then make your decision. Alternatively make your recommendation to the decision maker.

- direct training
- evaluation of training
- advising individuals
- advising managers and team leaders.

Trainers also take on a number of different roles when they are delivering learning or training events. The type of role they take on will depend on their individual style and will range from a trainer-centered to a learner-centered approach. This is shown in Figure 3.1.

In addition to the trainer-/learner-centered continuum a library trainer may take on a number of different roles during the course of a training program. Table 3.3 demonstrates the similarities and differences between the

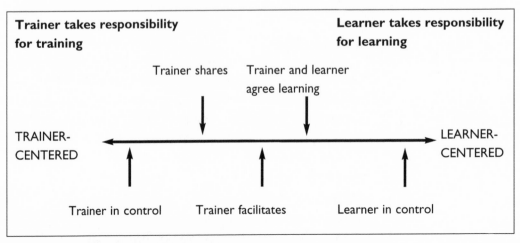

Figure 3.1 *Different approaches to training*

Table 3.3 Training roles

	Teaching	Training	Facilitating	Coaching	Mentoring	Counselling
Outcome(s)	To develop knowledge, skills and attitudes	To develop skills and behavior	To work through and reflect on a group or individual process to achieve an end result	To improve performance	To improve performance To develop career	To solve, resolve or dissolve a problem or issue
Who is involved	Teacher Student(s), Pupil(s)	Trainer Trainee(s)	Facilitator Group or Individual	Coach Client	Mentor Mentee	Counseller Client
Key characteristics	Group or 1:1 Didactic Teacher is an expert Teacher sets outcomes and directs process Emphasis on theory and practice Focus is on content rather than process	Group or 1:1 Didactic Trainer is an expert Trainer negotiates outcomes and directs process Emphasis on skills and behavior Hands-on approach Focus is on content rather than process	Group or 1:1 Experiential Facilitator is an expert in facilitation skills and may/may not be an expert in the content of the session Facilitator keeps process moving and keeps within group Normally confidential within group Focus is on process rather than content	Normally 1:1 Experiential Coach is an expert Coach and client negotiate a joint contract focused on a very specific aim Lots of feedback and encouragement Focus is on continuous improvement	Normally 1:1 Experiential Mentor is a role model Mentor is more experienced and "a few steps ahead" of the mentee Supportive, challenging, reflective relationship Normally confidential Focus is on work/career development	Normally 1:1 Experiential Counseller offers a safe space and process to work on specific problems or issues Normally confidential
Key skills	assertiveness skills assessment skills feedback skills listening skills motivational skills negotiating skills observation skills presentation skills questioning skills rapport skills reflection skills	assertiveness skills assessment skills coaching skills facilitating skills feedback skills listening skills motivational skills negotiating skills observation skills presentation skills questioning skills rapport skills reflection skills	assertiveness skills counselling skills facilitating skills feedback skills listening skills mentoring skills motivational skills negotiating skills observation skills questioning skills rapport skills	assertiveness skills assessment skills feedback skills listening skills motivational skills negotiating skills observation skills questioning skills rapport skills reflection skills	assertiveness skills feedback skills listening skills mentoring skills motivational skills negotiating skills observation skills questioning skills rapport skills reflection skills	assertiveness skills counselling skills facilitating skills feedback skills listening skills motivational skills negotiating skills observation skills questioning skills rapport skills reflection skills

different roles and also the difficulty in attempting to identify specific skills with specific roles – there are more similarities than differences between the set of skills required for each role. The skills that trainers require are considered in more detail in Chapter 4.

LOOKING AFTER YOURSELF

Health and fitness

It is very important that you look after yourself so that you are able to achieve a high quality training event. This really means being healthy and for the few days before a training event it is worthwhile being aware of and maintaining:

- a healthy diet
- a healthy lifestyle which involves exercise and appropriate levels of sleep.

It is also worthwhile reducing:

- sources of stress
- alcohol and other stimulants (tea, coffee)
- bad work habits, e.g., working extra long hours, long periods at the PC.

If you are presenting a paper or workshop at a library conference then there is always the danger that too much sitting around, too many meals, and too much networking in the bar may cause a lowering of energy levels! So it makes sense to pace yourself.

Resourceful states

The term anchoring comes from the field of knowledge known as neuro-linguistic programming (NLP) (see Garratt, 1997). Anchoring refers to a process that enables someone to change their state of mind at will. Anchoring is a natural process and depends on using personal original experiences, for example the question "where were you when you heard the news about Kennedy?" (or Princess Diana) is likely to bring back the total experience of receiving that news. Similarly mention of snakes or spiders will trigger off particular negative responses in some people. Positive associations may be triggered off by looking at vacation photographs, certificates, medals or trophies, or by thinking about a particularly positive experience.

This natural process can be harnessed to access any positive state of mind we need at any particular time. It is a technique which is very worthwhile as it helps the trainer to become more resourceful and flexible. The anchoring process involves:

1   Finding an appropriate environment, i.e., one free from distractions and interruptions.
2   Relaxing.
3   Recalling a time when you felt (confident, relaxed, powerful, humorous).
4   Stepping into that time in your imagination and feeling the feelings, seeing the sights and listening to the sounds. In this state you are fully associated with the experience.
5   Enhancing the quality of the experience, i.e., turn up the feelings, sounds and sights.
6   Once these are at peak then create an anchor, e.g., a unique touch or movement, sound or image.
7   Do something else briefly (this is called a break state).
8   You may need to repeat 4–7 a few times.
9   Test the anchor by using the unique touch, movement, sound or image.

Some key points about setting anchors include:

• It is often easier to learn this process by asking someone to talk you through it.
• Identify what you want to use as an anchor before you start the process – I find a touch on my knee or part of a finger works well (remember you may want to trigger your anchor in public).
• It is vital that you are fully associated with the process.
• The anchor is timed to coincide with full association with the original experience.
• This full association with the original experience is indicated by changes in breathing, posture, skin and muscle tone.
• This is a quick process and is likely to take less than a few minutes.

Energy

Training requires energy and trainers need to be able to maintain their energy levels throughout a training day or even week. There are a number of different techniques that are worth remembering if your energy begins to fall during a training day.

SEVEN ENERGY RAISING STRATEGIES

1   Take a five-minute comfort break.
2   Go outside. Jog for five minutes.
3   Drink some cold water.
4   Introduce some exercises, e.g., Brain Gym (see p. 18–19).
5   Put on some loud music and dance.

6   Make sure that you have some private time during the day, e.g., go for a walk, read a book, listen to a tape.

7   Have something healthy to eat, e.g., fruit or nuts.

Voice work

Voice work means techniques and practices that help you develop your voice. Ideas for voice work come from a number of different fields:

- theater
- martial arts
- music
- religion, e.g., Tibetan chanting
- Alexander Technique.

A key aspect of voice work is to practice using the voice in lots of different ways: from singing in choirs to singing in the bath, practicing chanting (ideal for people who don't feel comfortable singing), or practicing breathing properly. There are a number of trainers who offer specialist voice workshops.

SUPPORT FOR TRAINERS

Training can be a lonely business. This section looks at different ways of finding support either inside the training room, through working with another trainer (cotraining) or working with an assistant (training assistants), or outside the training room with a mentor.

Cotrainers

Cotraining involves working with another trainer either during the whole or part of a training session. There are three main ways of co-training:

- each person takes responsibility for particular sections of the program
- the two trainers deliver the whole program together
- a mixture of separate and joint delivery sessions.

The first approach means that each trainer is able to:

- play to their strengths by presenting and facilitating their own areas of expertise
- observe the group and learning process when they are not involved in delivering material
- have breaks from training.

This approach is commonly used in many different types of library training sessions.

EXAMPLE

A university library was introducing a new staff performance management program for all their 160 staff. This program was an in-house one designed jointly by the university's human resources department and library managers. As part of the change process the following series of courses was designed and delivered by one of the university's staff development officers working with one of the library managers. The program included the following different events:

- Introduction to performance management (2 hours)
- Performance management and me (6 hours)
- Performance management for managers and supervisors (6 hours).

Each event was codelivered and while the start and close of each session were jointly presented by the two trainers they then took it in turns to deliver their own sections. The trainers found that they were able to support each other during the training events. At times staff responded very negatively to the initial awareness session (Introduction to performance management) and the trainers found it invaluable having support. In addition, they were able to offer a united "university" perspective rather than one from their own department. They were also able to bring their own expertise to play and to present the subject with a detailed knowledge of both the library and university's situation.

The second approach where both trainers deliver the whole program is clearly described by Dina Lewis (1996) who was involved in delivering a series of team-building workshops:

The effectiveness of this collaboration was immediately apparent as we started to plan the first workshop. In the past the planning stage has been a lengthy and laborious process. I have formulated aims and learning outcomes slowly and painfully. This time however our combined attack quickly generated clear aims and objectives, new ideas for warm-ups and group exercises and a fluent and coherent structure to the session. Instead of the planning stage feeling like a trip to the dentist's it felt like fun: quick, stimulating and enjoyable.

The shared approach also encouraged a new readiness to take risks and try out new ideas. We both found the previous experience and repertoire of our co-trainer a great source of inspiration. Using each other's knowledge we extended our own resource bank of good ideas and practice . . . Supported and encouraged by each other, we shared our experience and generated new ideas to produce a program that was much more varied than either of us could have achieved individually . . .

We also found that a rapport developed between us that enabled us to take control and hand over control during a session. Instinctively we made the most of our own particular strengths and weaknesses. At any one time, quite naturally, we seemed to sense which of us was best suited to the task in hand. Our communication skills and styles seemed to complement each other's. Trainees commented on the success of our contrasting presentation styles. One trainee in particular said how annoying he had found co-trainers who behave as a double act. He congratulated us on avoiding that pitfall and said how unobtrusively we handled our changeovers.

One of the greatest benefits of co-training was the opportunity it gave us to talk things over. At any one time one of us led the session while the other was free to closely observe and monitor the responses of the trainees. On many occasions the observing trainer picked up non-verbal cues that may have otherwise been missed. It was fascinating to share insights and observations and compare strategies for dealing with tricky situations and the individual needs of the participants. Our conversations revealed that we had observed different reactions and behaviors during the sessions: this led us to a better understanding of the group.

Co-training these workshops proved to be an invaluable learning experience for us both. Although it could be argued that co-training is not cost-effective (why use two trainers when one trainer will do?), I would argue that it is an economic and effective means of delivering staff development within an organization. I have acquired many new skills, I find myself taking more risks and adapting more flexibly to the different needs of different groups. My presentation skills and communication skills have developed not least because of my improved confidence.

The third approach offers the opportunity to work together in areas where both trainers feel comfortable with the training material and to present their own particular sections too.

The major potential problem area with cotraining is the situation where the two trainers do not share the same values and beliefs about training and a power struggle ensues. This is damaging to the whole training experience both for the trainers and the participants as the focus shifts onto the trainers rather than the training material. Any differences of opinion need to be sorted out outside the training room.

5+ IDEAS FOR SUCCESSFUL COTRAINING

1   Observe your potential cotrainer in action before you agree to co-train with them. Are your training styles compatible? Do you have similar values and beliefs about training?

2   Talk to your potential cotrainer. Do you want to work together? What do you both want to gain from the experience of cotraining? Discuss your expectations. What are your concerns with cotraining?

3   If you decide to work together then you need to decide a plan of action. How will you share the work? Who will be leading each particular session/activity? How will you "hand over the reins" from one person to the other? If one person is leading a session when and how will the other person join in – by invitation, or "butting in?"

4   A key point to discuss is "what will we do if we disagree with something the other person has said or done during the training session?"

5   Another point to clarify is the role of the person not actually present-
    ing. Is it observing the group? Is it observing the trainer? Is it relaxing
    and having a break? Where do they sit – with the person doing the
    training, the group or outside the group?
6   How will you give each other feedback – at the end of each activity,
    in the breaks, at the end of the training event?
7   How will you celebrate your successful cotraining?

Training assistants

In information and library services individual trainers are often working by themselves in situations where they need to manage a large number of different factors ranging from lunch arrangements to individual
participants with special needs. Working with a training assistant gives
the trainer additional help and support while the person taking on the
role will have a unique opportunity to experience the training event.
Training assistants may be involved in some or all of the following
activities:

TRAINER

- Looking after the trainer and making sure that he/she has everything
  he/she needs.

PARTICIPANTS

- Clarifying questions arising from the course material
- Facilitating small group discussions
- Providing one-to-one support to people with additional needs, e.g.,
  someone with visual impairment.

HOUSEKEEPING

- Setting up the room
- Checking equipment
- Organizing refreshment breaks
- Dealing with incidental questions
- Collecting registration fees
- Handing out learning materials.

In some fields of training, for example commercial training programs, training assistants are commonly used as a means of providing excellent training programs. They are also commonly used in schools where paid support
staff provide help and assistance to the teacher. Their use in the library field
is currently fairly small. The author, who works as an independent trainer,

Table 3.4 *Benefits of training assistants*

Benefits to the trainer	Benefits to the assistant
There is someone there who is looking after and supporting YOU	You learn about the training process from a unique perspective
You can delegate many routine tasks leaving you to focus on the participants	You have an opportunity to learn more about the course content

regularly works with assistants who provide invaluable support. In addition, she works as an assistant herself: this provides free staff development and an invaluable insight into how other trainers train. The benefits are presented in Table 3.4.

7 KEY POINTS THAT MAKE WORKING WITH AN ASSISTANT WORK

1 Ensure that the assistant is a volunteer and really wants to help you run an excellent course.
2 Before you start discuss your expectations.
3 Make it clear what you want he/she to do and what you do not want he/she to do.
4 Spend time before the event briefing them.
5 During the event ask them for feedback.
6 Spend time after the event debriefing them.
7 Remember to thank them in an appropriate manner.

Mentors

Who do you talk to about your training activities? Where do you go for help? How do you plan your training practice personal development program? Mentoring offers a route to gaining additional support. Fisher (1994) has presented a useful guide to mentoring in information and library services.

Mentoring which is "learning by association with a role model" is an important way of gaining support in the following areas:

- specific skills or for a particular task or project
- training support and development
- professional contacts
- career and professional development.

Some organizations have formal mentoring schemes and these are typically aimed at new recruits and/or groups of staff who traditionally find barriers to their progress, e.g., women or staff from ethnic minorities. Informal mentoring schemes are very common and may be initiated by the mentee, their line manager or a colleague. Typically staff will indentify a mentor within their own organization but some workers, e.g., consultants, find it appropriate to approach a colleague in another organization.

As a trainer it is worthwhile identifying a mentor who is able to provide you with mentoring in association with your training activities. Phil Race (1995) describes the characteristics of mentors:

- someone we trust and feel we know
- someone whose views and opinions we respect
- someone who has our best interests and performance at heart
- someone who is willing and able to give us feedback
- someone who is essentially "on our side"
- someone who will help us plan our actions
- someone who will firmly (but kindly) keep our noses to the grindstone.

Essentially a mentor is a friend and someone who will support our personal and career development. Whether or not your organization has a formal mentoring program it is possible to identify and work with a mentor. If you are seeking someone to mentor you for your training activities then it is important to choose someone who is an experienced trainer and who remains up-to-date with new learning and training ideas. Phil Race suggests some tips on working with a mentor:

- choose someone you get along with and respect
- choose someone you feel comfortable with
- choose someone you have easy access to
- regard your mentor as a trusted friend rather than a teacher
- arrange definite meetings with your mentor
- agree upon targets with your mentor
- listen to your mentor
- share your learning problems with your mentor
- show your mentor that you value the support you receive
- remember to thank your mentor
- review your mentoring arrangement at least once a year.

You should think about the following questions before you start off on a training practice mentoring relationship:

- Why do I want to be involved in this relationship?
- What do I expect from this relationship?
- What concerns do I have about this relationship?
- How do I see the relationship working?
- How will we plan the outcomes of our meetings?

- How will we communicate between meetings?
- What will we do if the mentoring relationship is not working?
- What will we do if the mentoring process is not working?

EXAMPLE

Part of Tina's work included organizing and running in-house training events within her library which contained 15 staff. She had been doing this part of the job for two years and felt that it was working smoothly. After one training event on "Designing web pages" she received written feedback from one of the participants that was very negative about the training event and her role in the training process of the library. Tina was devastated. She did not feel that she could discuss it with her colleagues or team leader.

She decided to approach the training officer in her company and ask him for support. He agreed to meet her and they discussed the particular issue about the feedback. This helped Tina to get it into perspective. As a result of this meeting the training officer offered to be Tina's training mentor and together they identified an action plan which included:

- the training officer observing one of Tina's sessions
- the training officer and Tina reviewing her course design process.

As a result of this meeting, Tina felt that she could go on with her training role. She felt that there was a way forward, support for her development as a trainer, and someone with whom she could discuss training issues.

4
Key skills for trainers

INTRODUCTION

This chapter focuses on training skills and covers the wide range of skills (from assertiveness to reflection skills) that trainers require. These are all transferable skills and skills that library staff develop throughout their careers. The emphasis in this chapter is on exploring them in the context of training. In particular ideas from other fields, e.g., neurolinguistic programming, have been integrated throughout this chapter with specific examples from library applications.

Trainers need a range of key skills and those important for training include:

- assertiveness skills
- assessment skills
- coaching skills
- creativity skills
- counselling skills
- facilitating skills
- feedback skills
- listening skills
- mentoring skills
- motivational skills
- negotiating skills
- observation skills
- presentation skills
- questioning skills
- rapport skills
- reflection skills
- IT training skills.

Trainers use different combinations of skills depending on their circumstances, for example learning outcomes, type and size of group. In addition, each trainer will have a preferred style of working; this is sometimes described as a continuum from trainer-centered to learner-centered (see Figure 3.1). Effective trainers are able to move up and down this continuum depending on their specific training situation.

ASSERTIVENESS SKILLS

All trainers need to be assertive if they are to deliver high quality and high impact training events. Passive or aggressive trainers result in unhappy participants and unsuccessful training activities. Assertive behavior is linked to how someone feels about themselves and their particular situation.

If a trainer is working in a context where they do not feel very confident then the cycle shown in Figure 4.1 may take place leading to non-assertive behavior (either passive or aggressive depending on the personality of the trainer and the situation).

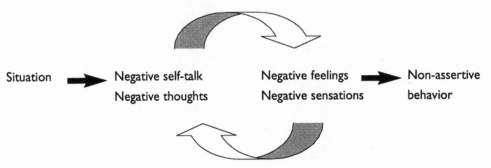

Figure 4.1 *Non-assertive behavior*

When trainers feel comfortable with themselves and confident in their abilities then the cycle shown in Figure 4.2 is likely to be taking place in the training situation and this results in assertive behavior being maintained.

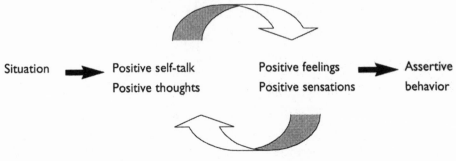

Figure 4.2 *Assertive behavior*

Assertive people:

- know what they want to achieve (their goal, outcomes)
- are aware of their own feelings

- are sensitive to others
- respect themselves
- respect others
- say what they think/how they feel
- give others the opportunity to say how they think or feel
- feel comfortable giving constructive feedback.

Assertive behavior can be identified through someone's body and verbal languages, as shown in Figure 4.3.

Body language	Verbal language
Open body language	Use "I . . ." statements
Relaxed	Use of clear statements
Calm	Use of positive statements
Good eye contact	Use of clear language
Standing square with feet on ground	

Figure 4.3   *Characteristics of assertive behavior*

ASSESSMENT SKILLS

Assessment is the process of making a judgment based on evidence.

This section is concerned with assessment as part of the training process rather than assessment as part of a certification process, vocational or academic qualification.

Why do we assess? Library trainers are constantly assessing their trainees and this often takes place informally. The reasons for this assessment include:

- to help support individual learning
- to provide feedback to the learner
- to provide feedback to the trainer.

The assessment can take many forms:

- what the trainee knows or can do at the start of the course
- to identify what the trainee is learning during the course
- to identify what the trainee is not learning during the course
- to identify what the trainee has learned by the end of the course
- to identify what the trainee has not learned by the end of the course
- to identify whether or not the trainee has achieved the course objectives/learning outcomes.

Assessment is an integral part of training and may take place at different stages in the training cycle. The different types of assessment are summarized in Table 4.1.

Table 4.1 *Types of assessment* (Adapted from Open University, *Identifying learning needs and assessing achievement*, People and Potential, Unit 2, 1994)

Type of assessment	When it takes place	Purpose	Outcomes
Initial/diagnostic assessment	Prior to or near beginning of a training program	To establish what a learner can do, or wants to do, or is required to learn Diagnostic	Identification of learning needs Decision to admit learner to learning program Assessment of prior learning (could lead to accreditation of prior learning)
Formative assessment	At an interim point in the training program	To review progress so far and give feedback to the learner To make an evaluation of the training given with a view to revising training plans in progress To provide learner support	Decision to continue or change course: • revise learning plan for individual • revise training plan for group
Summative assessment	At end of training program Assessment in the workplace	To assess an individual's achievement or proficiency To evaluate the success of training	Summative report on learner, often for accreditation Evaluation report on training program

The assessment process involves:

- identifying the criteria for assessment
- collecting the evidence from the learner(s), their peer(s) or their manager(s)
- making a judgment by comparing the evidence with the criteria – this judgment may be made by the trainer, a peer, self, manager or team leader, or an independent assessor
- giving feedback to the learner.

COACHING SKILLS

The concept of coaching is widely used in the worlds of sport and the arts where individuals may require coaching to help them to improve their skills and techniques. Coaching is also a useful means of enhancing performance in the workplace. Coaching sessions can be set up in the workplace or as part of a training event by agreement between individuals who want to improve their performance and someone who has the necessary skills to be able to coach them. The advantages and disadvantages of coaching are presented in Figure 4.4.

Advantages	Disadvantages
One-to-one process and therefore tailored to needs of individual	Time-consuming
Directly related to library's requirements	Requires skilled coach
Enhances relationship between coach and learner	
Learning is embedded into the work context	

Figure 4.4   *Advantages and disadvantages of coaching*

Coaching sessions may be used to help develop a wide range of skills such as:

- communication skills, e.g., ability to give feedback, presentation skills, ability to deal with difficult situations
- technical skills, e.g., ability to carry out information searches on a variety of online sources, media skills such as video editing
- trainer skills, e.g., starting and ending group sessions, managing interventions.

Cook (1994) describes the characteristics of a good coach as someone who is positive, enthusiastic, supportive, trusting, focused, goal-oriented, knowledgeable, observant, respectful, patient, clear and assertive. A coach will bring these skills together and use them appropriately throughout a coaching session.

Allan, Cook and Lewis (1996) have described the characteristics of a successful coaching session. These are grouped under four headings:

THE ARRANGEMENT

- is often voluntary
- the relationship is often one-to-one.

THE SESSION

- focuses on particular skills
- involves developing self-esteem and self-confidence
- provides an appropriate level of challenge
- the individual is stretched
- there is humor and fun.

THE INDIVIDUAL

- is motivated to learn
- responds positively to feedback
- is very active in the coaching session.

THE COACH

- models and demonstrates the required behavior
- provides abundant detailed feedback
- provides an emphasis throughout on learning and continuous improvement
- includes reflection on practice and learning
- knows when to withdraw.

EXAMPLE

Whetherly (1994) gives the following example of a coaching process:

A coach is preparing to train a new library assistant on the automated circulation system. To make the session most effective the coach will need to consider such factors as the knowledge and experience the library assistant has of such systems, what might be covered in the session and how the contents will be ordered, and also the date, time and venue, intervals between coaching, any necessary administrative arrangements, how the session will be reviewed, and what needs to be prepared in advance. Assuming a computer terminal is set up, the session may proceed as follows. The task is introduced and demonstrated to the learner, who is asked to explain it in her/his own words and then practice. When the learner has practiced sufficiently the coach might demonstrate at full speed and ask her/him to try again. All this might be related appropriately to another aspect of using the system . . . time and many skills are required in the coach. One key skill is the ability to give feedback on how the learner is performing, which will enable him/her to have a sense of progress – "You are accurate at this stage though you are not fast enough. You are following the procedure in the correct order." To reiterate, effective coaching is greatly dependent on the skills of the coach.

COUNSELLING SKILLS

One definition of counselling used by the British Association for Counselling (BAC, 1979) is:

> Counselling is a process in which a person occupies, regularly or temporarily, the role of a Counsellor and offers or agrees explicitly to offer time, attention and respect to another person or persons temporarily in the role of client. The task is to give the client the opportunity to explore, discover and clarify ways of living more resourcefully and towards a greater well-being.

Gerard Egan's three-stage model of counselling has become increasingly popular in the UK (Egan, 1990) and he suggests that effective counselling involves:

- exploration of the person's life situation
- the counsellor helping the client to identify a preferred problem-solving solution
- the client being helped to identify a problem-solving strategy to achieve this end.

Library trainers can find that issues arise during their training sessions that require counselling. This is particularly true with personal or management development programs. Sometimes a participant may request counselling or "time to talk through a problem." The trainer needs to make some important decisions at this stage:

- Do they step into counsellor role?
- Do they refer the participant to another agency?

The decision to step into a counselling role should be taken with great care and, preferably, after discussion with a mentor or line manager. A key question is: does the library trainer have sufficient skills, expertise and time to fulfill this role? Counselling is a professional task which requires specialist training and accreditation. If the trainer decides to step into this role then a new and explicit contract needs to be made with the participant.

Burnard (1991) describes some of the issues that can arise when trainers get involved in counselling:

- The trainer may feel obliged to change the trainee's work situation to ease pressure on them. While this may be a caring and humane thing to do, it has implications for the rest of the course, team and the library.
- The trainer may find that transference and countertransference (these are technical terms from the world of counselling – see Burnard, 1989) generated by the relationship may begin to affect the working and learning relationships. The trainer/participant and trainer/worker relationship may be changed. This may or may not affect the trainee's work performance.
- The trainer may adapt the training style and the content of the training program to accommodate the personal problems discussed by the student.
- Role strain may occur in both the training event and the library as delegate and trainer try to accommodate their new dual roles.
- The trainer may have difficulty in differentiating between their therapeutic and training roles.

Often referral to a specialist agency or counsellor is the best outcome.

EXAMPLE

As part of an ongoing training program that was anticipated to last a year an independent trainer facilitated an in-house staff development session at a local university. She anticipated that she would be involved in other aspects of this training program. At the end of the session, one of the trainees (a library team leader) came and asked for a word in private. She said that she was experiencing a number of problems at work and felt she was about "to go crazy" – would the trainer see her privately for counselling? The trainer gently explained that she was not a professional counsellor and would not be the best person to support her. In addition, it could cause conflict with her role as an independent trainer employed by the director of the library. The trainer agreed to e-mail this individual with information about local counselling agencies.

EXAMPLE

In the lunchbreak of a training event at a public library one of the participants asked for a private word with the trainer (a Director of another library). He explained that he was thinking of applying to work abroad and knew that this trainer had work experience in overseas information and library services. Could they meet up to discuss his ideas and would the trainer help him to make a decision? The trainer agreed to discuss the issue of working abroad with the participant and would see him for up to an hour the following month. The trainer made it clear that the participant would have to make his own decision.

CREATIVITY SKILLS

Libraries operate in a fast changing and complex environment. Change is inevitable and the ability to work with change is essential. Library trainers are often involved in change processes, for example the development and implementation of training events linked with the implementation of a new IT system or introduction of a new appraisal system. As change agents, library trainers need to offer:

- a proactive and constructive perspective
- an ability to work at all levels within the organization
- an ability to create constructive relationships
- an ability to diagnose current situations
- an ability to offer change process skills and experience
- relevant experience ("been there, done that")
- relevant and up-to-date knowledge
- facilitation, coaching and mentoring skills
- reflection skills.

Change agents are creative people who have the following characteristics in common:

- they are able to contact and enjoy silence
- they connect with and enjoy nature

- they trust their feelings
- they remain centered and functioning amid confusion and chaos
- they are childlike – they enjoy fantasy and play
- they self-refer – they place the highest trust in their own consciousness
- they are not rigidly attached to any point of view – although passionately committed to their own creativity, they remain open to new possibilities.

D. Chopra, *Ageless body, timeless mind*, Rider, 1993

Creativity involves making new ideas or putting together new combinations of existing ideas. One of the key differences between people who consider themselves creative and those who do not is that creative people consider themselves to be creative! Creativity can be enhanced by creating the right atmosphere for people to work in. Typically creativity requires an atmosphere which is:

- relaxed
- nurturing
- stimulating
- fun
- open
- honest
- safe.

Bentley (1996) identifies four creativity strategies:

- Visualization. Seeing the preferred future, or the ideal.
- Exploration. Using metaphors, analogies, or symbols to question assumptions and to jolt our paradigms.
- Combinations. Bringing various elements together in different ways.
- Modification. Improvising, adapting, adjusting what you already have.

There are many different approaches to creativity. A number of books on creativity are listed in Appendix A.

FACILITATING SKILLS

The word facilitator comes from the Latin *facilitas* meaning "easiness" and the verb to facilitate means to make easy, promote or help forward (an action or result). Facilitators of learning:

- believe that the learning relationship is one of facilitator and participant as equal partners
- believe that the learners have all the resources within them, i.e., their existing knowledge, skills and experience
- are centered on the learners and providing them with support
- create rapport with the learners

- see themselves as learners
- focus on the learning process
- encourage learners to participate
- are flexible
- ask lots of questions
- coach and support the group and individuals
- seek consensus solutions, win-win solutions
- work within a loose framework
- encourage lots of feedback on the training material, learning processes, group processes and trainer.

Facilitating individual or group learning involves managing the following processes:

- starting learning sessions
- climate building
- maintaining a creative environment
- working with individual and group processes
- consolidating, reviewing and evaluating learning
- ending learning sessions.

This is described in more detail with respect to groups in Chapter 10.

FEEDBACK SKILLS

Feedback is an important source of learning and it is an essential feature of effective training events. Ideally feedback takes place throughout the training event and it may be given by either the participants or the trainer. Feedback helps to produce improved performance and it is essential to maintain continuous improvement.

Feedback results in the person receiving the feedback learning more about themselves and this is often described using the Johari Window, as shown in Figure 4.5.

	Known to self	**Not known to self**
Known to others	Public self	Blind self
Not known to others	Private self	Unknown area

Figure 4.5 *Johari Window*

The aspect of a person which is known to others is split into the public and blind selves. Receiving feedback from others has the effect of increasing the size of the public self, i.e., the part that is not known to someone (the blind self) becomes smaller; this is shown in Figure 4.6.

	Known to self	**Not known to self**
Known to others	Public self	Blind self
Not known to others	Private self	Unknown area

Figure 4.6 *Johari Window: effect of feedback*

In a training context we often give feedback and one way of viewing feedback is as a gift. How do we package this gift? How have we thought about it, selected it and wrapped it up?

People have different tolerances for feedback and one useful way of thinking about this is through the metaphor of people as buckets, tumblers and thimbles. "Buckets" are ready and willing to receive feedback and may even seek it out. They are confident and want to develop. However, trainers need to be aware of "buckets with holes" as here nothing changes and the feedback goes through and out of the "bucket" without even touching the sides! In contrast "tumblers" are able to take in a small amount of feedback and are likely to respond to it. Finally, "thimbles" are likely to lack confidence and feel insecure. They may doubt their ability to improve and perhaps have an unhappy history of learning at school or in other settings. These people may only be able to receive a very small amount of feedback at any time.

Another helpful approach to packaging the feedback is to use the sandwich method. This involves presenting positive feedback, then a suggestion for change followed by another positive statement. A key point about the sandwich approach is that each part of the sandwich needs to be about the same size. An over-thick center can cause indigestion!

10 tips for giving feedback

1 Be clear about the purpose.
2 Start with the positive.
3 Be specific.
4 Refer to a behavior that can be changed.
5 Offer alternatives.
6 Be descriptive rather than evaluative.
7 Take ownership of the feedback.
8 Leave the recipient with a choice.
9 Give the feedback as soon as possible.
10 Think about what the feedback says about you!

10 tips for receiving feedback

1 Be prepared to receive feedback.
2 Listen carefully to the feedback that is given.

3 Look for the positive intention behind any negative feedback.
4 If you think the feedback is subjective or directed at your personality then use questions and ask for specific examples to discover the real issue.
5 If you think the feedback is vague then ask for a specific example.
6 If necessary then check it out with others.
7 Reflect on the feedback you are given.
8 Decide what you will do as a result of the feedback.
9 Give feedback on the feedback to the feedbacker.
10 Thank the person for the feedback.

LISTENING SKILLS

Active listening involves listening with our whole body and whole brain. Developing our listening skills improves performance in the following areas:

- obtaining information
- learning people's opinions
- exploring people's feelings and attitudes
- clarifying a misunderstanding
- assessing or appraising
- picking up small but perhaps very significant points of view
- demonstrating that you are actively involved and interested.

Table 4.2 summarizes the signs of active listening.

Table 4.2 *Signs of active listening*

Type of behavior		Signs of active listening
Body language		open stance
		lean forward
		appropriate eye contact
Nonverbal noises		mmmm
		hhmmm
Verbal language		
	Reflecting	"Let me see if I've got your point . . ."
	Supporting	"Yes, that's a good idea . . ."
		"And then?"
	Constructing	"Would it help if we . . ."
		"What would you like to happen . . ."
	Clarifying	"Are you saying that . . ."
	Interpreting	"So you seem to be saying that . . ."
	Confirming	"So, we agree that . . ."
	Testing	"Would it be right to say that . . ."
	Summarizing	"So, your group appears to have identified the main issues as . . ."

Table 4.3 *Meta programs 1 (Adapted from Ted Garratt, The effective delivery of training using NLP, Kogan Page, 1997)*

Name	Overview	How to identify them	How to help them
Toward/away			
Moving toward	People who have clear goals in mind. They want to be at the training event and want to start working toward their goal. They are good at managing priorities. They have trouble identifying problems.	Have a clear goal in mind. Speak from an "I" position Will use phrases like "Let's do it" Will talk about benefits, achievements, goals, etc.	Work together to create goals and objectives Show how the training will help them to reach their personal goals Use incentives not threats Remove blocks from their way
Moving away from	People who focus on problems. They are motivated to solve problems. They have trouble keeping focused on goals. They may say they have registered for the course to get away from the workplace.	Will not have a clear goal in mind Will talk about things they want to avoid Will use passive language Will talk about problems Will not jump into action at the start of an exercise and will follow or react to someone's lead	Use words like "solve," "prevent," "there won't be any problems" Be clear about what they do and don't want from the training Look ahead for any potential problem areas Help them to clarify their objectives
Possibility/necessity			
Possibility	People who are focused on possibilities tend to be positive, enthusiastic and eager to try new things.	Will tell the trainer what they want to do Will believe they have control for themselves Interested in new possibilities, choices and options Will see potential in new materials Will use words like "wish," "want," "possibility," "can do" Will talk about doing things Will talk about a strong future focus	Help them to see the opportunities for learning, growth or change Help them to see how they can apply what they have learned Don't tie them down to a rigid set of instructions Use words like "choice," "possible," "different," "alternatives"
Necessity	These people are here because they feel that they have no choice. They are not looking to get anything out of the training. They want to survive it. They prefer traditional ways of learning.	Will be closed in their nonverbal communication Will sit back and wait for things to happen May "go through the motions" Will want to overanalyse everything Will use words like "must," "have to," "need," "should," "ought to" Will give evidence of not being in control of their life Will not like new options	Show respect for input they know Show respect for their views Fully explain anything new Be highly structured and systematic in explanatory exercises Be specific regarding the outcomes from learning Use words like "proven," "known," "correct," "right way"

Table 4.4 *Meta programs 2 (Adapted from Ted Garratt, The effective delivery of training using NLP, Kogan Page, 1997)*

Name	Overview	How to identify them	How to help them
Self/other			
Self	People who are very self-oriented are very self-absorbed and pay a lot of attention to their own thoughts and feelings.	Tend not to show emotions Tend to pick up on what is said rather than how it is said Sit back and reflect Don't spot what is happening around them Not highly skilled in people skills Don't reveal much emotion on their faces	Keep the input focused on specifics Show them you understand them Give them space Don't try too hard to build a relationship with them Do be very clear about what is being said Do not get too drawn into them
Other	These people are very sensitive to others and quickly establish relationships with other course members. They will quickly pick up on the feelings and needs/wants of others.	Show emotions Will respond to what is said and also how it is said Will give a lot of eye contact and nod in agreement Will be aware of how others are responding and feeling Will look around the room to check others out May come up to the trainer at the end and thank them/ask them how they feel	Be expressive in communicating Show enthusiasm for the group Circulate and mix (during course and in breaks) Ensure all of group understand before moving on Show rapport, empathy and respect for the group Show how materials can be used with others Talk about how others have used materials
Options/procedures			
Options	These people love choice and will like to have a range of possible options available to them.	Will look for options and choices in the material Will search out new possibilities If they are given a procedure to follow then they are likely to change it, i.e., develop their own option They will use words like "option" and "choice"	Offer choices and options Ask them to come up with alternatives Use phrases such as "the options are . . ." or "you can choose . . ." Treat their variation on your exercise with respect
Procedures	These people prefer to follow a set procedure and, if a procedure is not available, then they will design one.	Will follow established procedure Will ask for a procedure if one isn't offered Answers the question "why" by telling "how" it happened Will tell a story by telling the order in which something happened	Offer them clear procedures and guidelines Don't offer them too many choices (it causes overload) Use phrases such as "the rule is . . ." "the right way . . ." and "first . . . then . . . finally . . ." Give them time to tell their "procedural" stories

Table 4.5 Meta programs 3 (Adapted from Ted Garratt, The effective delivery of training using NLP, Kogan Page, 1997)

Name	Overview	How to identify them	How to help them
Same/difference			
Same	These people tend not to like change and find it hard to adapt to new skills, techniques or ideas. They are unlikely to initiate change. They often stay in the same job or library for a long time.	Will look for how the materials, ideas, etc., are similar to the ones they are familiar with Will look for familiar themes Will use words like "same," "similar," "common," "like" Will look for other people who agree with their views Will talk about the past Will be diffident about accepting new ideas	Emphasize similarities between the new materials and the old Show how new skills and ideas build on the past Show areas of commonal ground Show that you are both working to the same goals Build upon their past experiences
Difference	These people love change, new ideas and innovation. They change jobs or organizations frequently. They need constant change and challenge.	Will look for what is new or different in materials Will look for errors and omissions Will look toward the next steps and the future Will not want to dwell on the past	Highlight new ideas and skills Show how new ideas will lead to change Show them how they will be different Use innovative training techniques Use words like "new," "innovative," "unique," "never been done before"
General/detail			
General	These people will look for the big picture. They like ideas and concepts. They may become bored with details.	Will ask for overview or big picture Will enjoy discussing concepts and ideas Will enjoy roving from idea to idea Will not follow through all the detail Will not refer to many details Will not want to dwell on the past	Start with the big picture and overview Don't go into too much detail too soon Watch for them becoming bored Use a variety of training techniques Use words like "big picture," "concept," "framework," "generally" Be prepared for them to make big leaps with ideas and respond accordingly
Detail	These people prefer information to be broken down into specific and logical steps. They will only form conclusions if all the data is available. They need very specific instructions and lots of very good examples.	Will talk about lots of details Will ask very detailed questions Will use lots of adjectives and adverbs	Present materials in a logical way Don't be too theoretical Use words like "detail," "precisely," "exactly," "specifically," "first," "second," "third," "schedule" Get them to draw up an action plan to implement their learning

Table 4.6 *Meta programs 4 (Adapted from Ted Garratt, The effective delivery of training using NLP, Kogan Page, 1997)*

Name	Overview	How to identify them	How to help them
Internal/external			
Internal	These people go inside themselves to check their emotions, e.g., whether or not the course is going well or whether or not they have done a good job. They won't accept negative comments, e.g., about the quality of their work, if they feel inside that they have done a good job.	Ask them "How do you know you have done a good job?" They will answer with reference to themselves and their own feelings. Will tend not to seek or give feedback Will use words like "I know" and "it feels good" Will not reveal very much through their facial expressions or gestures	Show them how the material fits with their standards, values and beliefs Show them you respect their point of view Use phrases like "try it out and decide for yourself" Help them to clarify their own thinking
External	These people require feedback and input from other people and outside sources. They tend to be heavily influenced by the thoughts and opinions of others. They decide their own view by how others respond.	Will look for comparisons with other people to form a view Will check their views and ideas with others on the course Will ask the trainer "is this right" or "am I going in the right direction" Will use phrases such as "they say" or "everybody knows" Will tend to look for approval Will require lots of praise and support	Let them see what other people think and do Give them lots of praise and feedback Get them to check their responses to exercises with others Check who they are using as authority and then build on it Use phrases like "a recent article in the . . ." or "X says . . ."

Table 4.7 *Meta programs 5 (Adapted from Ted Garratt, The effective delivery of training using NLP, Kogan Page, 1997)*

Name	Overview	How to identify them	How to help them
Convincer metaprograms			
Automatic	These people will base their judgments and make decisions on very small amounts of information. They will leap to conclusions without bothering to wait. They often find it hard to change their minds.	Will immediately accept what you say and begin to think about applying it	They are likely to become bored as you work through the materials in more detail – provide variety in materials and techniques
Consistent	These people are never really convinced and need to reevaluate materials time and time again. Often they will go back to an earlier point and start again.	Will constantly ask questions challenging basic ideas Will refer back to material already covered and reopen old discussions	Accept that they may never be convinced by your materials Respect their questions and questioning Use them to help build up a very robust session
Number of examples	These people need to see, hear or do things a number of times before they are convinced. The majority of people with this pattern need to hear things three times. Hence the old training adage "tell them what you are going to tell them, tell them, and then tell them what you have told them."	Will need to see or hear new materials a number of times Will ask for other examples	Make sure you cover new materials a number of different times using a number of different techniques Use more than one example (ideally three)
Period of time	These people need time (a few days or weeks) before they accept and are convinced by new materials.	Will say "I need time to think about it"	At the end of sessions say "some of you may need time to think about these ideas" Include follow-up activities after the end of the course

EXAMPLE

A team leader in a public library, Jan was asked to run a series of training programs on managing challenging customers. She thought that the first program had gone well and was surprised that a number of people said that she had covered the material too quickly. They would have liked more examples of each situation. One person said that he found the course boring as he couldn't bring in his own ideas and the exercises were like "painting by numbers." Other people commented that they thought the exercises were very clear and helpful.

Jan brought back this feedback to her mentor (Caroline) who had recently discovered the ideas about metaprograms. They decided to use the metaprograms to discuss the session. During their discussion they found out that Jan's own metaprograms in a training context were automatic and procedural. She felt silly if she said something more than once and was worried about not having sufficient time. She thought it very important that everyone followed all the exercise instructions otherwise "they would get it wrong."

On reflection, she realized that not everyone in the group would have an automatic convincer so that most people would need to see/hear the new ideas a number of different times. She also discovered that not everyone wanted to follow instructions precisely. Some learners were motivated by discovering options and different ways of doing things.

As a result, Jan decided to review the training materials and find new and different ways of presenting key ideas. She would start asking the group to suggest other ways in which the new ideas could be applied to the workplace. She decided to maintain her clear instructions for exercises and be more flexible with people who varied the exercise.

NEGOTIATION SKILLS

[Note: This section is adapted from training materials provided by Realization at Stenhouse, 1998.] Trainers are likely to use their negotiation skills at different stages of the training process. At the planning stages they may need to negotiate with their employers to gain agreement on running and participating in the training event. If a library professional group has asked them to run a particular training event, for example at a conference or seminar, then they may need to negotiate the arrangements. Working with cotrainers and training assistants often means that negotiation skills are required so that everyone can come to a positive agreement about the organization of the event. Sometimes, negotiation skills are required with individual participants or whole groups.

The overall negotiation process involves the following stages:

- prepare
- discuss
- propose
- negotiate
- agree
- action plan.

5+ factors for constructive negotiations

1   Use a positive approach. Separate the personality from the problem. Widen your horizons. Look for a joint solution not a battle.

2 Set the meeting up to be constructive. At the beginning, summarize the purpose in positive terms. Avoid words like "try to come to an agreement/decision."

3 Use a problem-solving approach. Identify their needs. Ask what they want.

4 Involve them in the process of reaching a conclusion. Use "we" and ask "how may we . . . "

5 Show your willingness to accept the other person's point of view. Use statements such as "I can see . . . "

6 Finally, if others are taking a WIN–LOSE or LOSE–LOSE approach then

- Help them to save face.
- Put your irritation away in a corner for later.
- Acknowledge the positive intention behind the action.

Tips for preparing for a negotiation

THINKING ABOUT YOU

1 Know your desired outcome. Use a SMART objective (see pp. 152–4). Make sure your outcome is phrased in the positive. Think in the wider sense. (What would happen if I didn't achieve my desired outcomes? Is there only one way to arrive at my desired outcome?)

2 Know why you want it. Know what you don't want.

3 Know your limits.

4 Know your bargaining counters.

5 Know your strengths and weaknesses.

6 Know your ideal, realistic and fallback solutions.

7 Be aware of the balance of power.

THINKING ABOUT THEM

8 What might they want?

9 What might their limits be?

10 What might they be prepared to bargain with?

11 What are their strengths and weaknesses?

12 What might be their ideal, realistic and fallback positions?

13 How much power do they have compared to me?

THINKING ABOUT THE CONTEXT

14 What is their organizational culture?

15 What are their organizational norms?

16 Do you need to be aware of any legal, factual or operational considerations?

17 What is their negotiation history, and how will it have an impact on these negotiations?

THINK ABOUT THE ENVIRONMENT

18 What will be the best physical layout for the negotiations? How will chairs be arranged? Who will sit near whom?
19 Is there a history of negative or positive meetings in the room?

12 tips for putting your case effectively

1 Look and sound confident.
2 Dress for success.
3 Be assertive.
4 Build rapport.
5 Soften disagreement.
6 Keep it positive.
7 Do not imply blame.
8 Be aware of your own power.
9 Harness your own voice.
10 Think about the positive not the negative outcomes.
11 Remember they may need something from you.
12 Have breaks when necessary – they will give you time to think.

5+ behaviors that help the negotiation process

1 LABEL AND GUIDE THE OTHER PEOPLE

Always say what you are going to do as:

* it draws attention to you
* it allows them to hear the whole of the message
* it gives you more time.

For example:

"I'd like to ask a question. I . . . "
"I'd like to make a suggestion. I . . . "
"I'd like to clarify something. I . . . "

2 TEST UNDERSTANDING

This is a very useful technique which:

* enables you to check that you understand the key points
* makes sure that everyone else understands

- gives you the opportunity to restate the problem in your own words
- acts as a slowing mechanism.

Use phrases such as:

"Can I just check . . . "
"Let me make sure I've understood this fully . . . "

3 SUMMARIZE

Use this technique:

- mid-discussion
- when agreement is reached.

4 TAKE TIME TO THINK

- Ask questions until you fully understand their position.
- If necessary ask for time to think.
- "Comfort" breaks give time out and an opportunity to gather your thoughts.
- Give nonverbal signals to show you are paying attention.
- Use filling phrases.
- Reflect back.
- Summarize.

5 PAINT A PICTURE OF HOW IT COULD BE

Use phrases such as:

"Suppose we . . . "
"How would it be if . . . "

Questioning techniques for negotiations

1 CHUNKING UP

This means moving to a higher (more abstract) level. It is useful to gain agreement at a high level and then chunk down to sort out the details:

- What will X mean to you?
- And what will that mean?
- And how will that affect you?
- What is the bigger picture?
- What is this an example of?
- What are your aims?

- What is this part of?
- What is the wider purpose?
- For what purpose?

2 CHUNKING DOWN

This means moving down to a more specific level. It involves asking very detailed questions:

- what?
- how?
- when?
- who?
- where?

Examples include:

- Can you expand on this?
- Give me more detail.
- What exactly do we need?
- What is involved/steps are necessary?
- Give me some examples.
- What specifically?

Challenge assumptions. These are identified by "must," "should," "ought," "never." Use a "soft-front end." Challenges include:

- What would happen if we did?
- What would happen if we didn't?

3 USING QUESTIONS CREATIVELY

To gain commitment:

- Do you agree . . . ?

For feedback:

- What is your view?
- How do you see it?
- Are you happy with?

To float an idea:

- How would you react to . . . ?
- Have you ever thought about . . . ?

To stop negativity/anger, ask for more information:

- What has happened?
- Can you explain it to me?

To clarify:

- Where does this fit in?
- What does this relate to?
- Where might that take you?
- Can you clarify?
- Give me another/different example.

40+ tips for successful negotiations

1 Look behind the position.
2 Invite criticism or advice.
3 Redefine any "attacks" on you as attacks on the problem.
4 Avoid attack/defense exchange.
5 Avoid *irritators* – value judgments and statements which glorify the options you favor.
6 Separate intent from behavior.
7 Label suggestions and questions.
8 Use *I* language rather than accusing.
9 State your reasons for first making your proposal.
10 Maintain genuine curiosity.
11 Don't let trust become the issue.
12 Set the direction of the process.
13 Let them set the direction of the process.
14 Focus on gathering information that you want.
15 Focus on gathering information about the other's proposal and/or feelings.
16 Focus on changing the other's position.
17 Focus on understanding the other's position.
18 Use more open than closed questions.
19 Manage flow of information views and opinions.
20 State expectations.
21 State incentives.
22 Identify common pressures.
23 Build on common ground.
24 Don't negotiate if you are overpressurized.
25 Don't negotiate if you are preoccupied with something else.
26 Don't negotiate if you are inebriated.
27 Be open.
28 Be honest.

29 Assume trust.

30 Listen more, talk less.

31 Ask questions for clarification.

32 Summarize issues in a neutral way.

33 Ask others to explain issues item by item.

34 Watch and listen for signals – and respond.

35 Look for clues to *their* priorities.

36 Be congruent.

37 If you get stuck then do something different.

38 Don't negotiate with yourself in front of the other. If an option is raised and you need more time or information ask for a break or schedule another meeting.

39 If you get stuck then stop doing what you are doing, generate at least three different options for doing something else, choose the best and go with it.

40 Remember to keep your body language open and your feet on the ground.

OBSERVATION SKILLS

Observation skills help a trainer to pick up information about the participants and their physical, emotional and intellectual responses to the training materials, the training process, the other participants and the trainer's own performance. They enable you to pick up and respond to small changes, e.g., in physiology. The topic of observation skills has been extensively developed in the study of NLP (see O'Connor and Seymour, 1994 or Garratt, 1997). It is divided into three areas:

- sensory acuity
- perceptual positions
- peripheral vision.

Sensory acuity

Sensory acuity or sensory awareness is the ability to notice the minutest changes in a person's physiology. Fine tuning our sensory awareness means you begin to notice more and more how people change from minute to minute. This is a very useful skill for a trainer as it enables you to monitor with greater accuracy what someone is experiencing. It is also useful when you want to identify how someone is responding to an idea you may be presenting. To begin with it is useful to notice these physiological differences. Take a snapshot in your mind. Then calibrate these clues as the training event progresses.

VISUAL CLUES

Facial signals include skin color and tone, lower lip size and pupil dilation. These all change from second to second. Another important indicator is breathing. Is the breathing deep or shallow? How fast do they breathe? Are they holding their breath at any time? Body language also gives vital clues. Is the body pose open or closed? Are the arms crossed against the chest or are they in an open position? Are the hands clenched or open? Are there any fidgeting movements? Is the hand shaking or still? Are there any foot movements or are the feet still?

AUDITORY CLUES

Listen to the tone and timbre of the voice. Is the pace fast, well paced or slow? Does the voice sound relaxed or is it tense? Listen out for verbal indicators such as sighs, groans or grunts.

Perceptual positions

The ability to move into and look at a training event from a number of different positions gives a trainer increased flexibility. One approach to this process was described by O'Connor and Seymour (1994) and it involves three different positions:

- **Position one** This is your own reality. Your view of the training event as the trainer.
- **Position two** This is what it looks like from another person's point of view. This is understanding and accepting another person's perspective without necessarily agreeing with it.
- **Position three** This is the view from the outside, the impartial observer.

Using different perceptual positions is a useful skill for trainers, for example before starting the training session or while it is in progress.

BEFORE STARTING THE TRAINING SESSION

Use the different perceptual positions as you set up the room. Go to position one where you will be working from during the day. Assess this position. Then move to position two, for example by sitting in different delegates' chairs. What is the perspective from here? Do you want them to have this view or a different one? Then move into position three by moving to the edge of the room – be "a fly on the wall." What is the perspective from here?

MONITORING THE PROGRESS OF THE TRAINING EVENT

Use the different perceptual positions at different times during the training event. Consciously check out your own position one. Then move to position two, for example by imagining the view from a delegate. What is the perspective from here? Do you want them to have this view or a different one? Then move into position three (either physically or mentally) by moving to the edge of the room. What is the perspective from here?

Peripheral vision

Moving from focused into peripheral vision has a number of effects on a trainer:

- they can see the whole group at any time
- they are likely to become more centered and calm.

When you are leading a training event it is worthwhile spending time in peripheral vision and, if you are not familiar with this technique, then it requires practice. A simple technique for going into peripheral vision is to focus on an object at the other side of the room. Relax and defocus your eyes. Gradually expand your vision so that you become aware of what is on the current edge of your field of vision. Remember to keep your eyes relaxed.

PRESENTATION SKILLS

Presentation skills are the skills required to prepare and deliver presentations. The preparation process for presentations is covered in detail in Chapters 6 and 7. The delivery of a presentation may be enhanced in a number of different ways:

- by being prepared
- by using body language
- by using verbal language
- by using Satir categories (described later in the chapter)
- by using stage anchors.

Being prepared

The more prepared you are,
the less worried you'll be.
The more prepared you are,
the more effective you'll be.
The less prepared you are,
the more worried you'll be.
The more worried you are,

the less effective you'll be.
If you are going to be more effective,
it's important not to worry.
If you don't prepare,
you will worry.

K. Kalish, *How to give a terrific presentation*,
American Management Association, 1997

Being prepared involves thoroughly researching and designing your presentation, taking into account ideas presented in earlier chapters. Then it involves practice. If possible practice your presentation in the room in which you will be delivering it. If this is not possible, then rehearse in a room of a similar size and acoustics.

Rehearsals are best carried out in front of an audience, perhaps friends and colleagues at work. If no audience is available then consider video or audiotaping yourself. Some people (including the author) rehearse in front of family members and pets!

Using body language

Ideally your body language needs to be open and to demonstrate your enthusiasm, interest and motivation.

6 GOOD REASONS FOR GESTURING

(Adapted from K. Kalish, *How to give a terrific presentation,* American Management Association, 1997)

1 It lets off nervous energy.
2 It makes you more interesting to watch.
3 It makes you look more relaxed and natural.
4 It adds emphasis.
5 It adds emotion, interest and vocal variety to your voice.
6 It can be used to illustrate what you are saying.

Hand and arm gestures are a useful way of emphasizing and marking what you are saying. For example, a phrase such as "in the future" can be marked by a movement of the right hand forward and to the right while the phrase "in the past" is marked with a movement of the left hand to the left and slightly backwards. These movements, sometimes called analog marking, add another dimension to presentations and help to make them richer and three-dimensional.

7 POSITIONS TO AVOID

(Adapted from K. Kalish, *How to give a terrific presentation,* American Management Association, 1997)

Some trainers suggest that these positions should be avoided while others disagree and suggest that it is up to individual trainers to find their own style.

1 Female fig leaf with arms crossed over chest.
2 Male fig leaf with hands over genitals.
3 Both hands deep in pockets.
4 Soldier standing at ease pose – feet shoulder-width apart with hands clasped behind.
5 Hands on hips or pointing finger at audience.
6 Open wound – one hand across chest holding opposite upper arm.
7 Putting a hand in a pocket without first making sure it doesn't contain keys or money which will jingle.

Preparing yourself

This topic is covered in Looking after Yourself in Chapter 3.

Using verbal language

When you are rehearsing your presentation check that you are using simple language and short sentences. Practice using different tones (see Using Satir categories below), pace and emphasis. For example, read one of your sentences in a number of different ways and check out the impact of different emphases.

EXAMPLE

Read this sentence as it is written below emphasizing the word in italics. Notice the effect.

Project management involves six different steps.
Project management involves six different steps.
Project *management* involves six different steps.
Project management *involves* six different steps.
Project management involves *six* different steps.
Project management involves six *different* steps.
Project management involves six different *steps*.

Using Satir categories

How do we make our training sessions interesting and include a range of speech patterns and mannerisms? One approach to adding variety is to use what are known as the Satir categories, named after Virginia Satir, an American family therapist. There are five categories or ways of being:

- blamer
- placator
- computer
- distracter
- leveller

and they are described in detail in Table 4.8.

Table 4.8 *Satir categories*

Satir category	Description	Verbal language	Body language
Placator	The placator is always trying to please, apologizing, never disagreeing (no matter what).	"Whatever you want I'll do." Whiny voice.	Body in low position. Often one side lower than another.
Blamer	The blamer is the fault finder, a dictator, the archetypal boss. S/he acts superior.	"You never do anything right." "It's all wrong." The voice is hard, tight, shrill and loud.	Aggressive body stance. Points. Hands on hips. Heavy breathing.
Computer	The computer is very correct and very reasonable. There is no sign of any feelings. S/he is cool, calm and collected.	"If one was to calculate the time, one would work out that it isn't possible to carry out the plan in the time allowed." The voice is dry, monotone and the words are likely to be abstract.	The posture is straight-backed, motionless, with no sign of life below the neck.
Distracter	The distracter will often produce an irrelevant fact or anecdote. This may be very entertaining although some people may find it irritating.	The distracter may introduce stories or snide comments with phrases such as "I must tell you . . .," "You'll be interested to hear . . . ."	Posture involves lots of movement, e.g., fiddling, twisting buttons, moving bits of paper.
Leveller	The leveller is an assertive, coordinated and integrated position. Body, voice and mind are all working together.	Levellers will use clear language such as "What we are going to do next is . . . ," "Does anyone have any comments to make?", "I feel uncomfortable with that comment . . . ."	Body language is well balanced and integrated. They stand on both feet with an appropriate use of body language.

The relevance of the Satir categories to training is that by introducing minute doses (sometimes only for a few seconds) of each of the different categories then you offer variety and interest to the audience. Ideally the trainer is always in leveller mode but may want to dip into the other categories, for example while describing something or while telling a story or anecdote. This is a strategy used by many great speakers and comedians. Comedians often move into one of the five Satir categories and then exaggerate it.

It is helpful to practice the Satir categories, for example at home or on social occasions, and then introduce them to your training sessions.

Using stage anchors

Trainers have the training room as their stage and by using different parts of the room/floor for different purposes can build up powerful anchors or triggers in their audience. For example, if a trainer tells a joke from a specific spot in the room and then returns to that part of the room and tells another joke then the audience will, at an unconscious level, link that part of the room with jokes. The next time s/he goes to that part of the room they will be expecting and receptive to a joke. Effective trainers often use physical space in a very specific manner.

Stage anchors can also be linked to the learning cycle (see Chapter 2) and different stages in the training event (see the 4MAT approach in Chapter 7). Two examples are given in Figures 4.7 and 4.8. In Figure 4.7 the anchors were used by a trainer running an assertiveness course and in 4.8 by a library manager making a presentation to her staff of 67. She was giving them bad news. The difference in space between each distinct location in Figure 4.8 was very small (less than ten feet).

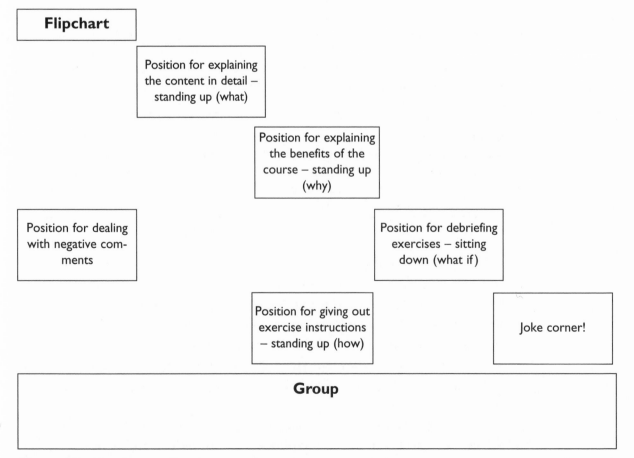

Figure 4.7   *Use of stage anchors in an assertiveness course*

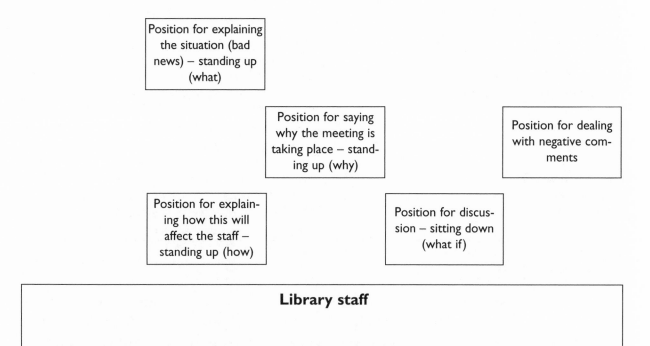

Figure 4.8   *Use of stage anchors in a presentation*

QUESTIONING SKILLS

Questioning is an important trainer's tool. The appropriate use of questions may be used to:

- manage the session
- facilitate the process: bring people in, move the group forward, take a new direction
- obtain information and ideas
- follow a line of thought, gain responses and bring potential issues to the surface
- open up a subject, develop new ideas, bring in people's experiences, explore other angles, make connections and new links
- clarify a problem or issue
- find out somebody's requirements.

Used appropriately, questioning can have an impressive effect on the learning process. Some important do's and don'ts for asking questions are given in Table 4.9.

Specific questioning skills

OPEN AND CLOSED QUESTIONS

Open questions are likely to open up possibilities and show that the trainer is open to ideas, feedback, etc. Conversely, closed questions limit possibilities.

Table 4.9   *Do's and don'ts for asking questions*

Do	Don't
Ask questions	Make statements
Ask one question at a time	Ask multiple questions
Make it clear whether you are asking one person or the whole group	Ask questions that may be rhetorical, aimed at an individual, and/or the whole group
Ask open questions	Ask leading questions
Ask short questions	Ask long rambling questions that are complicated and lead people to wonder what is the point of the question
Be open to the answer	Be closed to the answer
Remain neutral to the answer	Judge the answer – "that's right" or "that's wrong"
Be prepared to listen	Expect the participants to read your mind and come up with "your" expected answer

THE META MODEL

The study of communication that is called neurolinguistic programming has developed a model of questioning called the Meta Model. This offers a series of questions which helps a trainer to reverse/unravel the distortions, generalizations and deletions which people often make when they are communicating something. They enable people to develop a greater understanding of another person's map of the world. The model is described by Garratt (1997).

The Meta Model can be used for:

- gathering information
- clarifying meanings
- identifying limitations
- opening up choices.

The questions are based on the use of:

- what?
- where?
- when?
- who?
- how?

Notice that the model doesn't involve the use of *why* as this question sets up a loop. For example, it often results in someone justifying themselves and their actions. In a training context *why* needs to be used cautiously as it may create tension and a sense of someone being judged.

Using the Meta Model

The Meta Model questions are presented in Table 4.10. At first sight, you will see that there is a lot of information presented in this table. The suggestion is that you start playing and practicing with specific

Table 4.10 *The Meta Model*

	Example – in a training group a participant says:	Challenge – the Meta Model question	Result	Language patterns
Deletions	I'm fed up	With whom?	Recovers lost noun	Unspecified that is ambiguous
	We aren't communicating	How specifically are you not communicating? Who is not communicating with whom?	Recovers specific information about the experience/process	Unspecified verb – verbs that delete something that is done
	Training is a good thing	How is training a good thing?	Turns noun back into verb and recovers the deleted process	Nominalizations – verbs made into nouns
	They don't listen to me	Who doesn't listen to you?	Recovers to whom/what it refers	Lack of referential index – pronoun is not specified which deletes to whom/what it refers
	Work-based learning is more effective	More effective than what?	Recovers the standard for comparison	Comparative deletion – the standard of comparison is deleted
	This is the way it should be done	How do you know? Who says?	Recovers source of opinion or belief	Lost performative – value judgments, rules and opinions where the source is missing
Distortions	They don't care about me	How do you know? What leads you to believe that?	Recovers source of information	Mind reading – assuming you know another person's views
	Training drives me mad	How do you let training drive you mad?	Recovers the imagined process of the causal connection	Cause and effect – belief that one person's action causes another's emotional state
	If you knew how tired I was you wouldn't ask me	How do you know I don't know? How do you know you're tired?	Recovers the presupposition	Presuppositions – basic assumptions that must be true for the model to make sense

Table 4.10   *Continued*

	Example – in a training group a participant says:	Challenge – the Meta Model question	Result	Language patterns
Generalizations	He's a manager – he'll find the course easy	How does being a manager means he'll find the course easy? Has anyone who is not a manager found the course easy?	Challenges the complex equivalence and opens up new options Recovers the imagined process	Complex equivalence – where two experiences are interpreted as the same: A=B
	She never listens to me	Never? What would happen if she did?	Recovers the exceptions and counterexamples	Universal quantifier – generalizations such as all, every never, everyone, no one
	I have to finish this tonight	What would happen if you didn't? Or else?	Challenges the rule and explores the consequence	Modal operator of necessity – words that imply a general rule such as: should, shouldn't, must, must not, have to, need to, it's necessary
	I can't do this exercise	What prevents you? What would happen if you did the exercise?	Challenges the rule and explores the consequence	Modal operator of possibility – words that define what is possible such as: can't, can, will, won't, may, may not, possible, impossible

examples and gradually expand your repertoire. There is no need to remember the specialized terminology although some readers will be fascinated by this approach to structuring language. The key point about the Meta Model is to use the following process:

1 Listen to what is being said to you.
2 Repeat it to yourself.
3 Ask yourself "what's missing?"
4 Ask yourself which question will help your clarity.
5 Ask the question and discover what happens.

You will see from the table that the Meta Model could be used to alienate, irritate and upset people! This is not the intention. Use it with rapport (see below) and soften your questions inserting "a soft front end." Examples of soft front ends are given below:

- "I'd really like to understand this, so, what exactly do you mean by . . ."
- "Sorry, it may just be me, but how is it that X means/causes you Y . . ."
- "This is new to me, is this always the case?"
- "I don't quite understand the connection. Would you mind explaining X again . . ."

RAPPORT SKILLS

Rapport skills enable you to build and maintain a positive climate and they work at both an individual and group level. If two people are communicating with each other and are "on the same wavelength" then they are in rapport. There are a number of very specific signs which indicate when people are in rapport, for example their facial expressions match each other and their verbal language has similar rhythms and tones. Here are some of the signs of being in rapport:

- achieving a harmonious and understanding relationship
- feeling at ease and comfortable with the other person
- being on the same wavelength
- seeing eye to eye with the other person
- feeling in tune with the other person.

Building rapport

The ability to develop rapport is a crucial communication skill and it enables us to motivate others. In some cases we find rapport develops naturally with someone while in other cases we have to work at developing it so that we can work comfortably and effectively with the other person.

There are two main benefits of becoming more aware of rapport and rapport building skills: with practice we can develop these skills and choose when to use them, e.g., in a situation when rapport is "lost"; and we can also develop an unconscious level of competence and so become more adept at using rapport-building skills in everyday situations.

Rapport is a process and, like any process, can be learned. People who are very good at getting on with others are actually saying and doing things that will help them to generate that rapport. They may not be aware of this process which may be taking place at an unconscious level. Rapport takes place when two or more people are matching each other's body and verbal language. It can sometimes appear that people in rapport are "dancing," as they take turns to lead and follow each other in their conversation. Rapport takes place when people have naturally similar physiology, language and/or common experiences or make efforts to match them.

Physiology matching

One simple way of increasing rapport is to match someone's physiology and some of the things you can match are:

- overall posture, e.g., leaning backwards, standing up
- crossing and uncrossing of limbs
- gestures, e.g., shaking finger
- rate of breathing
- facial expressions, e.g., smiling, frowning
- rate of blinking.

This is something we all do naturally to some extent. With practice, it is possible to become excellent at creating rapport through matching physiology and this then becomes an unconscious habit. It is easiest to start by matching one characteristic and then add in others. With practice this will start to happen naturally. Some do's and don'ts for matching physiology are shown in Table 4.11.

Table 4.11   *Do's and don'ts of matching physiology*

DO	DON'T
Be respectful	Match in a gross manner – this can look like mimicking and is insulting
Be subtle – match small movements or movements in one part of the body, e.g., hands	Match every movement the other person makes
Behave in a way with which your body is comfortable	Match in ways that you feel personally uncomfortable with
Match parts of the body which you feel comfortable with, e.g., match their arm movements with your arm movements and not the rest of the body	Match someone who is in a very distressed state – otherwise you may pick it up. (In this situation you may want to match small movements as a means of creating rapport.)
Match small subtle movements rather than huge movements	
Move with the rhythm and flow of the conversation	

Language matching

Voice matching is a useful way of developing rapport and it involves matching the following verbal clues:

- volume
- tempo
- rhythm
- pitch
- tone
- length and choice of phrases and sentences
- choice of key words and phrases (including jargon)
- use of language to indicate thinking style
- use of language to indicate metaprograms

As with body matching, it is worthwhile starting by matching one characteristic and then adding in others. With practice this becomes easy and will start to happen naturally.

Matching common experiences

On any training event all participants are likely to start off with a number of common experiences:

- they are library staff
- they will have arrived at the training venue and, perhaps, had refreshments
- if they all work for the same organization then they will have many things in common, e.g., recent restructuring, parking problems, new director, excellent cafeteria
- if they all work in the same sector then they will have other things in common, e.g., new government legislation to contend with, takeovers and mergers, new IT facilities.

These common experiences can be used to build rapport at the start of the training event and this involves using inclusive language. Use of inclusive language enables everyone present to feel included in whatever statement(s) the trainer is making, i.e., no one is excluded by language.

EXAMPLE

Start off the session with statements that match everyone's experience:

"Good morning. Here we are on this training session in Boston. I'm pleased you were all able to find the hotel. Some of you may have travelled by car while others will have used public transport or walked here. Some of you have already found the bagels and coffee and if you haven't yet had any then help yourself to refreshments – they are at the back of the room."

EXAMPLE

The author recently attended a training event aimed at staff in public libraries. One of the visiting workshop facilitators introduced herself with "I'm XXX. I've never worked in a public library (thank goodness) and don't know anything about them. I work in the retail sector. It's completely different from your situation and this workshop worked well for our store managers. I'm sure it will work well with you." It didn't!

How much better if she had introduced herself in the following way: "Hello, I'm pleased to be here at your conference. It's great to see so many of you here in Baltimore today. The coffee was a welcome starting point! I'm very interested in running the workshop today. I come from the retail sector and we have many characteristics in common with public libraries. We serve the public, work under lots of pressure and we are often open long hours! I look forward to us all sharing our ideas and experience and learning from each other."

Pacing and leading

Pacing and leading is an important skill for trainers as it enables them to lead individuals or the whole group. It involves matching someone for a while and then pacing them until you have gained rapport (see Figure 4.9). If you then slowly change what you are doing (offer a lead) then the other person will follow you. It only works if you have good rapport and don't rush the process. If your level of rapport is sufficient then the other person will unconsciously match you. If they don't follow your lead then it is a sign of insufficient rapport.

Pacing and leading individuals involves creating rapport using physiology, language and experience. Pacing and leading groups involves the same process and, in particular, pacing and leading the energy and pace of the group is a useful means of creating and maintaining rapport.

MATCH ⟶ PACE ⟶ PACE ⟶ PACE ⟶ PACE ⟶ LEAD

Figure 4.9 *Pacing and leading*

REFLECTION SKILLS

Thinking about and reviewing are both activities that help to improve performance either on training courses or in the workplace. Reflection is a key part of the learning process and this is demonstrated in the learning cycle that was presented in Chapter 2 and is repeated here in Figure 4.10.

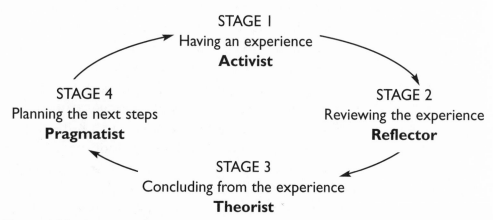

Figure 4.10 *Learning styles*

Reflection involves questioning, criticism, analysis and evaluation either during an activity and/or at the end. Reflection is an essential activity in all training events – reflection by participants will enhance their learning and it is an essential route to professional development and improved performance for trainers.

Reflection can be recognized in the trainer's process skills, in their ability to:

- ask questions, e.g., who, what, why, how
- shift focus, e.g., from one theoretical perspective to another, from the general picture to a point of detail, from the task to the individual to the group
- switch from content to process (and vice versa)
- identify the learning styles of themselves and others.

In general these process skills can be summarized as the ability to move around the process and content in a flexible manner. Finally, reflection can be observed in the use of the language of reflection, which has the following characteristics:

- it is open
- it offers theories, ideas, guesses
- it invites feedback, questions, suggestions
- it is questioning
- it is cooperative rather than competitive.

Building reflective activities into the structure of your training events will help to ensure their success.

Reflection-in-action and reflection-on-action

Reflection-in-action is the process of reflecting while the learner is working on task. It is a short-term activity and the findings may be used to improve the quality of the outcome of the task.

According to Morrison (1995), reflection-in-action tends to be an instrumental activity, which is focused on the immediate task (and its set of routines, strategies or practices) as a means of improving the outcome. As a trainer, encouraging reflection-in-action as participants are working through activities and exercises can enhance their learning.

The use of a longer term lens through reflection-on-action enables the learner (participant or trainer) to look back on a completed task, for example a case study, exercise or whole training event and question, analyse, criticize, and evaluate both the theoretical models and the actions involved in the task. The outcome of this process may then be used to inform the next stage in the process.

Reflection can be encouraged during training events by trainers providing:

- an environment for reflection
- activities to help reflection.

Ways of providing an environment for reflection

ALLOCATING TIME TO REFLECT

The process of reflection is often squeezed out of everyday learning activities when trainers are eager to include a lot of content. It is essential to allocate time for reflection. This time may be allocated during or at the end of a learning process. Time for reflection needs to be built into the training event so that it is seen as an integral part of the learning process rather than an extra.

ALLOCATING SPACE

The physical environment is also important if meaningful reflection is to take place. A quiet and nondistracting environment is important if learners are to focus on their findings in a thoughtful manner.

DEVELOPING PSYCHOLOGICAL SPACE

Participants need to feel psychologically comfortable and, in particular, confident and unthreatened if they are to be able to work reflectively in a meaningful manner. Some kinds of reflection, e.g., on issues such as career development, may raise emotional issues for the learner.

FOCUSING REFLECTION

There are three different approaches to focusing the reflective process during learning sessions:

- trainer/learner where the trainer works directly with a learner and guides him or her through a reflective activity
- learner/another learner where learners help each other to reflect and learn from their activities
- learner/self where the learners focuses on their own activities and reflects on them in a structured way.

The advantages of either the trainer or another learner being involved in the reflective process is that the use of external information allows another perspective to be taken into account by the learner. It helps the process become more objective.

CAPTURING IDEAS

Learning logs and diaries have evolved as a means of capturing the outcomes of reflective practice. These are described in Chapter 11. Alternative forms of recording reflective practice may include the use of tools such as mind maps or media such as audiotapes or video.

MODELLING REFLECTIVE BEHAVIOR

Modelling reflective behavior will help learners to incorporate reflection into their everyday learning activities. Trainers may:

- reflect aloud on the learning process
- refer back to a previous session in a reflective manner
- ask for feedback as a means of explicitly reflecting on a particular activity/event/issue
- reflect and ask for comment on their own performance and practice.

Activities to help reflection

DEVELOPING A SERIES OF QUESTIONS TO PROMPT REFLECTION

Pre-prepared sets of questions may be used to prompt reflection. These could be very simple questions such as:

- why?
- what?

- how?
- what if?

These questions could be offered at a more sophisticated level by asking learners to note their preferred questions and develop their use of other questions. Apparently, there is a link between the questions a learner asks and their preferred learning style (see Chapter 2). The question "Why?" indicates a reflector, "What?" a theorist, "How?" an activist and "What if?" a pragmatist.

USING QUESTIONS TO ENCOURAGE A CHANGE OF FOCUS

Questions may also be used to help the learner to develop their perspective on a particular subject or activity. Typical questions may ask learners to change their focus from

- a very detailed analysis to a broad picture
- identifying similarities to identifying differences
- self to others
- the people to the task
- content to process

or vice versa. The metaprograms (see Tables 4.3 through 4.7) offer an approach to helping people change their focus.

USING HONEY AND MUMFORD'S LEARNING STYLE MODEL

Knowledge of the use of learning styles is helpful when planning reflective activities so that these are set up to cater for them. When learners know their preferred learning style (reflector, theorist, activist, pragmatist) then this information may be used to help them to improve their reflective practice, e.g., activists may find it difficult to reflect and want to move on to the next task/activity and by reminding them of this factor they may find it easier to remain on task.

REFLECTING ON EMOTIONS

In some learning situations, e.g., group work or when dealing with emotionally charged themes, it is useful to enable learners to identify and reflect on their emotions. These need not be emotionally charged or cathartic events; sometimes a simple statement will enable the staff to develop their awareness of the emotions in a particular learning situation. A statement such as "Think back to the feelings you had when you started the team-building activity and note how they changed during the course of the activity. Notice how you feel now and whether or not you need to do something to help you to focus on the next part of the session" will help the learner to reflect on their emotions.

DEVELOPING THEORETICAL MODEL(S)

Reflective practice may be used to help learners to develop their understanding of theoretical model(s). For example, learners may be developing their understanding of different models of society, or the development of theories of scientific research, and the reflective process can be used to help them to develop their understanding of these model(s) and, perhaps, the relationship of their experimental work to a particular paradigm. This may involve the following processes:

- identifying assumptions
- separating assumptions from data
- linking with similar/different models
- using a range of theoretical perspectives.

USING PEER LEARNING

Pairs and small group activities are a useful way of encouraging reflection. For example, participants can work in pairs with one person acting as the questioner while the other reflects on a particular activity. The questioner has prepared a form listing questions and notes down the responses. The pair then reverse roles and work through the exercise again.

EXAMPLE

A practical "Planning the future" in-house staff training event that was aimed at library managers included the following activity which encouraged reflection. The following exercise was started during the training event:

1 Staff worked in pairs. One person (A) described a particular problem. The other manager (B) asked questions to promote reflection. The discussion was audiotaped.
2 One week later (A) listened to the audiotape in the presence of a third manager (C) and (A) developed a mind map from what s/he heard. (C) then asked questions to encourage (A) to reflect further on the problem and then come up with a series of actions.
3 (A) then informed his/her manager of his/her intended actions.

The exercise was set up so that the three people only worked with each other once during this process. The exercise encouraged learning transfer from the course into the workplace, it encouraged team building and it encouraged reflective thinking.

The exercise was devised by a trainer whose preferred learning style was reflector!

TRAINING SKILLS FOR IT

Information technology may be used as a learning resource, i.e., to support the learning of particular material, or as the actual content of the training program. Its use as a learning resource is covered in Chapter 6.

Many library staff are involved in teaching IT skills to their colleagues or to their customers. These events take many forms from individualized instruction through to group training sessions.

IT training sessions are like any other training session and the guidelines for running learning group sessions apply with IT teaching too (see Chapter 10). Some people are nervous about attending IT training sessions so it is worth while remembering to create rapport with the participant(s) and an environment conducive to learning.

Many IT rooms don't have training tools, e.g., flipcharts, whiteboards, so it is worthwhile double checking these when you are organizing an IT training session.

A variety of training activities can be used in IT training sessions:

- brainstorming
- mini presentations
- paired working
- games or quizzes (paper-based or online)
- small group work, e.g., solving problems
- exercises, e.g., filling in a worksheet
- open learning packages (paper-based or online)
- question and answer sessions
- discussions.

A number of specialist resources provide guidance on teaching IT skills in information and library services, for example Hollands (1999) provides ten ready-to-run workshops for teaching the Internet to library staff. Biddescombe (1996) provides a useful overview of training for IT with many useful surveys and questionnaires.

EXAMPLE

Pressler (1999) describes an interactive staff training process for electronic library access that includes a diverse range of activities such as lecture-style sessions, discussions, hands-on sessions, "Website of the Week" service, access to online learning materials, e-form feedback and evaluation process.

The sessions cover the following topics:

- HTML basics
- HTML advanced
- File management
- Constructing searches
- Retrieval effectiveness measures

- Internet subject gateways
- Intelligent agents
- Electronic journals
- Internet resources for Arts
- Web architecture.

EXAMPLE

Helmut, an information worker, attended an "Introduction to SPSS" workshop. This workshop included the following activities:

- introductory lecture using PowerPoint slides
- informal quiz to check knowledge of basic statistics and jargon (pairs exercise)
- open learning package (to introduce the SPSS)
- case study
- discussion
- question and answer sessions.

In addition, the trainer offered an e-mail support service as a follow-up to the event.

5
The participants

INTRODUCTION

This chapter considers the participants or course attendees and is divided into five sections:

- know your learners
- working with cultural diversity
- working with library staff and customers
- working with students
- working with people with special needs.

Libraries are located within a culturally diverse society. Themes and issues that need consideration when thinking about designing and delivering inclusive training events include gender, sexuality, ethnicity, religion, cultural differences, people with disabilities and people with individual circumstances, for example HIV-positive, in a caring role. Three particular groups of learners are considered here: library staff and customers, students and people with special needs.

KNOW YOUR LEARNERS

Research into your participants starts when you start planning the training event. The more information you have about them and their requirements then the easier it will be for you to design an effective training program. One approach to learning more about your audience or group is to find out as much as possible about them by:

- talking to the learners
- talking to their team leaders/managers
- talking to their training officer.

The following checklist provides an outline of the types of areas that need to be explored. This information can then be used in the course design stage (see Chapters 7, 8 and 9) and also during the training process (see Chapter 10).

Checklist of learner characteristics

(Adapted from J. Gough, *Developing learning materials,* IPD, 1996)

DEMOGRAPHIC FACTORS

- Number of learners, their age and gender
- Cultural background
- Personal disabilities/special needs
- Location(s) – where they work, where they live
- Jobs
- Professional experience

MOTIVATION

- Why are they learning – organizational change, change in working practices/job responsibilities?
- What are the learners':
  – needs/goals/expectations?
  – hopes and fears?
  – feelings about the proposed training event?
- What level of motivation and confidence do they have?
- How can the proposed training materials/activities relate to their work?
- Have they ever experienced this type of learning before?
- Do they need support?

SUBJECT KNOWLEDGE/SKILLS

- How do they feel about the subject being studied?
- What is their current level of skills?
- Have they any misconceptions/inappropriate habits?
- What past experience/personal interests are relevant?

LEARNING FACTORS

- What are their beliefs about learning?
- What learning styles do they prefer?
- What learning skills do they have?
- What experience do they have of the proposed training method?

- Are there likely to be any problems using particular types of learning materials/activities?
- Are there any problems/issues arising from their attendance at the course with other members of their team/library?
- Are there any relevant family/social factors?

TIMESCALE

- Is there a timescale for the learning process?
- What time will they have to learn at work or in their own time?

WORKING WITH CULTURAL DIVERSITY

> When we speak of cultural diversity in the workplace, we're not just speaking of nationalities or ethnic groups, but also of age, gender, race, religion, sexual orientation, physical abilities, where you live (metropolitan/small town/rural locations), plus subcultures within any of these categories based on occupation, education and personality.
>
> S. J. Walton, *Cultural diversity in the workplace*, Irwin, 1994

How do libraries respond to working with cultural diversity? What are the implications for them and their training practice? This section focuses on cultural diversity within a training context and explores two main topics: training practice and reviewing our training practice.

Many information and library services in the public sector, and also some in the private sector, offer staff development programs that look at working with cultural diversity. As a trainer it is worth while attending one of these programs as they will provide you with information on the rationale and organization context for equal opportunities work.

Typically, these programs include the following topics:

- introduction to the theme
- relevant legislation
- organization's policies and practices
- exploring discrimination in practice
- difference issues and the library
- working together
- implications for you.

Garrett and Taylor (1993) provide a useful guide to equal opportunities training.

Do's and don'ts on training courses

(Adapted from: H. Garrett and J. Taylor, *How to deliver equal opportunities training*, Kogan Page, 1993)

Do's

1 Avoid stereotypes in case studies and examples.
2 Use both "he" and "she" (or "they").
3 Use pair and small group work to increase the opportunity for everyone to participate.
4 Occasionally elect spokespersons for group feedback who are not from the majority group of course participants, rather than always allowing self-selection.
5 Challenge discriminatory language or behavior, explaining why you are doing so.
6 Be a role model for participants in your language and behavior.
7 Think about what you say and do – what impact will it have on the different people within the group?

DON'TS

1 Use examples where all managers are male and all shelvers or library assistants are female.
2 Use gender-specific terms.
3 Use too much large group work where a few individuals may dominate and others may find it difficult to join in and actively participate.
4 Use participants as spokespersons for the whole of their gender or race, e.g., "Jane, you are a woman manager, tell us how women managers feel about . . . " or "Bushra, as a Muslim, what do you think these readers likely to want?"
5 Jump down people's throats if they use out-dated expressions about equal opportunities issues. Participants need to know how and why language has changed.
6 Allow offensive anti-equal opportunities statements to be made on the grounds that training courses are confidential and people should be allowed to air their views. People need to be free to question and clarify their own beliefs, but not at the expense of others.
7 Be drawn into colluding with a small group of participants.
8 Expect to be universally popular!

Communication skills

A key factor that enables the inclusion of all course participants on a training event is the trainer's communication skills. Rapport is a key skill and is described in Chapter 4. Many library staff who work with diverse groups develop specialist communication skills such as learning sign language or learning second or third languages to meet the needs of particular groups of people. Whatever the needs of the participants Walton (1994) provides the following guide for clear communication in culturally diverse contexts:

1   Speak clearly.
2   Avoid slang expressions.
3   Avoid insider jokes.
4   Avoid acronyms.
5   Condense your communication to main points.
6   Refrain from extraneous explanations and elaborations: they can be confusing.
7   Repeat your main points.
8   Speak correct English.
9   Use a visual accompaniment and handouts.
10 Note nonverbal clues of confusion rather than asking "Do you understand?"

EXAMPLE

On a recent communication skills course in a commercial company the trainer used a long metaphor about a selection box and this was enjoyed by the group of librarians, information scientists and knowledge managers. At the end of the metaphor (which was a very humorous one) a Dutch librarian said, "It sounds hilarious but I don't know what a selection box is." There was an unhappy pause as the trainer and the group realized that she had been completely baffled by the story and associated jokes. As a result she felt left out of the training activity.

Reviewing our training practice

The EduLib materials (see McNamara and Core under "Sample Training Resources" in the Appendix) provide excellent guidance on reviewing training events and although they were written with academic librarians in mind the information is relevant to all library trainers.

"Walking the talk" is a way of reviewing the workshop and relating it to the circumstances in which librarians teach.

Entry to the program or event
Do the advertising methods encourage all people within the target group to apply for the activity or program, irrespective of gender, age, marital status, sexual preference, disability, part-time and full-time status? Language and visuals are an important aspect in ensuring inclusion rather than exclusion.

Barriers to entry
Does the way in which we have organized the program present any barriers to access for particular groups of people? One potential exam-

ple could be the timings of sessions. There is no one convenient time for any teaching session, but it is important that we review what we are doing and take account of comments that are made by potential participants.

Selection to the program

If we have a program that is oversubscribed, on what basis do we select participants? This need be no more than on a "first-come first-served basis," but it is useful to be explicit about the criteria.

Learning design

Have we taken account of the needs of learners based on the assumption that learning and the ways in which we learn are different for different individual learners? Do we use different theories of learning to help us provide a relevant mix of activities? How active is the learner?

Learning materials

Is the language of the case studies, etc., free from gender bias? Do our case studies and examples appropriately reflect all learners? We need to consider the mix of feminine and masculine subjects within case study material – issues such as, for example, is it always a man cast as the senior figure within a case study, are we always using women in case studies portraying emotional difficulties? We can make case studies neutral in terms of casting names, as letters of the alphabet, or our cases can challenge stereotype assumptions. When presenting information we can turn the usual labels around and say she/he rather than he/she. Are we providing examples which are acceptable across cultural boundaries? Whatever our choice, it is important to revisit our assumptions and review our style of presenting information to ensure that we are inclusive rather than exclusive when working with groups.

Finally good practice within an equal opportunities context has a direct correlation with good teaching, training and facilitative practices. While it is important to review our equal opportunities practice, this aspect should be seen as an integral part of providing an effective learning experience and not as additional work.

WORKING WITH LIBRARY STAFF AND CUSTOMERS

Library staff and customers regularly attend training events run by library staff. There are a number of special points worth noting.

Library staff as learners

Library staff are as culturally diverse as any other group of people. The checklist presented under the heading "Know your learner" is relevant to both in-house and external trainers who will be working within the library profession. At the planning stages of the training program it is worthwhile obtaining as much information as possible about the staff, their expertise and experience.

The type of library has an impact on the training program as staff from different environments, for example academic, public, workplace are all working in different organizational cultures and with different pressures. If you are working with staff from different types of libraries then it is important to balance the range of examples to cover the experiences of all the participants. A biased session with examples from just one library sector will lead to disgruntled participants. If you are asked to provide a training event that will be attended by library staff from different sectors then it is worth while carrying out additional research to ensure that you understand the different contexts and respond to different needs.

Different groups of library staff work in very different situations, e.g., full-time, part-time, permanent, temporary. Their work and educational experience vary hugely and this needs to be taken into account when designing training events (see the example in Chapter 4, Questioning skills). It is also worthwhile thinking about how they will apply their learning into the workplace as some staff may find it hard to obtain time to consolidate and practice new skills. This means that this part of the learning process needs to be firmly embedded in the training program. For example, in some information and library services there are large numbers of part-time workers and this group of participants may find it difficult to practice new skills and techniques outside of the training program as they are always scheduled to work on busy service points. They will be required to use their new skills immediately and, possibly, without support. In this type of situation consolidation and integration of new skills have to take place during the training event and the participants will find it useful to be provided with comprehensive training materials that they can use as reference tools in the workplace. Goulding and Kerslake (1997) discuss training for part-time and temporary workers.

If you are a trainer working within your own organization then you start with the advantage of knowing the participants, the culture and issues of the library, and the relevance of the training event to the organization. However, there are some potential problems that can arise as your colleagues:

- may not take you seriously
- may not take the event seriously
- may gang up against you
- may take the opportunity to bring up issues or problems not relevant to the training event.

This can be handled in a number of different ways – by clarifying your role at the start of the training event and by gaining clear agreement about the subject matter for the day. It is useful to write down/record the desired learning outcomes and display them. This means that if issues or problems arise that are not relevant to the day's agenda then it is simple to refer back to the agreement drawn up at the start and say that they are beyond the scope of the event.

If colleagues do gang up on you then they are best dealt with assertively (see Chapter 4), by challenging their behavior and making a clear request that they work within the parameters set by the training event. Humor is an invaluable tool here! Hopefully, the majority of librarians are particularly supportive of their colleagues.

Customers as learners

Library patrons may attend workshops or presentations led by the library staff. Normally patrons attend voluntarily so that you know they are keen to come along and learn. It is worthwhile remembering that your patrons:

- do not know library jargon
- may not feel comfortable in a learning role
- will need to adjust to you "wearing a different hat."

All the facilitative processes described in Chapter 10 are useful in helping customers to feel comfortable in this particular role.

WORKING WITH STUDENTS

Library staff in formal education settings (schools, colleges and universities) have traditionally provided skills training sessions for students on a range of topics from general library awareness through to advanced Internet searching skills. Factors that affect these programs include the following:

- Library staff may have no control over the timing of the program, e.g., they may be part of a general orientation program which takes place while the new students are still becoming acclimated to their new environment. Some students may be confused, lost, overwhelmed, homesick, panic-stricken, ready to give up, i.e., the reptilian part of their brain has taken over. Other students will be completely in control of their situation and relaxed, confident and focused on learning.
- The number of students attending the session. In some universities groups of 100 students are scheduled into introductory sessions.
- Student motivation. Depending on the stage of their studies, students are likely to vary in their motivation to learn information, research, IT or media skills.

- The students will come from a diverse range of backgrounds with varying skills and expertise.
- Students will come from a diverse range of cultural backgrounds. Some students will have little experience of U.S. educational practice and may expect very formal teacher-centered sessions (see following section).
- Some students will have additional needs (see final section in this chapter).

Library staff are involved in a wide range of training programs for students and these may vary from basic library skills programs through to advanced programs for doctoral students. While some of these needs are met through one-time training sessions others require a variety of services. Barry (1997) writes about the needs of doctoral students and suggests that the following multifaceted approach is taken to teaching information skills at the doctoral level:

- a portfolio of services which offers different services to different users
- individual one-to-one tutorials in addition to group sessions
- instruction that transcends the common technical "how to use systems" approach and incorporates advanced skills training on how to optimize use
- opportunities for self-help delivery of training as a supplement to formal programs
- training in context of academic subject (rather than generic training)
- training that attempts to target the needs of particular users at their time of need, after orientation
- training that takes into account individual learning styles
- training that develops mental models of complex information systems in the minds of users
- training that convinces users that there is something to learn and the effort required is worthwhile.

Culture and behavior

Every national culture has its own values and norms and if the experience of participating in a training event does not match or even clashes with these then it is difficult to learn. As with individual learning styles, it is worthwhile learning about these cultural norms as they provide valuable information for the design and delivery of training events.

The following model is commonly used in university-based library training programs as a means of helping library staff appreciate cultural differences and take them into account in the planning and delivery of

training sessions. Hofstede (1980) identifies four dimensions for considering cultural differences:

- power/distance
- uncertainty/avoidance
- individualism/collectivism
- masculinity/femininity.

POWER/DISTANCE

Power/distance relates to the level of inequality within an organization. If this is high then traditional boss–worker relationships will exist while if it is low then the boss–worker divide is smaller. These inequalities may be in relation to money, status, power or rights.

Countries that have a high power/distance culture tend to value autocratic styles of management: employees are expected to conform and do as they are told. Conversely, countries with a low power/distance culture value independence, working together and mutual respect. Countries which display a high power/distance culture include Spain, Hong Kong and Iran while those that are characterized by a low one include the USA, Germany and Italy.

The implication here for trainers is that participants from countries with a high power/distance culture are likely to favor traditional teaching and training styles rather than learner-centered approaches. If the course design doesn't take into account this difference then the training program may not be successful.

UNCERTAINTY/AVOIDANCE

The uncertainty/avoidance dimension refers to the extent to which different cultures cope with uncertainty or ambiguity. Cultures with a high level of tolerance to uncertainty/avoidance are comfortable with breaking the rules, dealing with ambiguous situations and taking risks. Examples include France, Spain, Germany and many Latin American countries. Cultures with a low tolerance welcome clear rules and procedures, enjoy established processes and take fewer risks. Cultures with a low to medium level tolerance to this dimension include Australia, Canada, the UK and USA.

The implication here for trainers is that participants from countries with a high uncertainty/avoidance culture are likely to enjoy exercises and activities that involve complex problem-solving and taking risks. However, these approaches will not match the needs of people from cultures with low uncertainty/avoidance dimensions. The course design needs to take into account this difference or it may not be successful.

INDIVIDUALISM/COLLECTIVISM

Individualism/collectivism describes the relative individualistic or collectivistic culture in particular countries. Countries that are highly individualistic include the U.S. and UK and this contrasts with countries such as Greece, Iran and Turkey which have a collectivistic culture. Individualistic cultures welcome and respect individuals' rights to query, criticize and question while collectivistic cultures expect individuals to subsume their needs to "the greater good."

Again, trainers need to be aware of these differences when planning learning events for groups that are culturally diverse or groups from either high or low individualism/collectivism cultures. Individuals from a collectivistic culture are likely to feel uncomfortable with the idea of debating and criticizing ideas with their trainers whereas people from an individualistic culture expect these activities. Similarly, it is likely that people from these different cultural backgrounds will have different approaches to giving feedback to their trainer or on the course. This will have an impact on the way they complete course evaluation forms.

MASCULINITY/FEMININITY

The last dimension is masculinity/femininity and this is based on stereotypical notions of the two aspects: masculinity includes assertiveness, rational-logical thinking and competitiveness, and femininity includes nurturing, people-focused, intuitive and emotional behavior. High masculine societies include Germany, Japan, the UK and USA, while high feminine cultures include Scandinavian countries and the Netherlands.

As with the other three dimensions, the masculinity/femininity one should have an impact on the design and delivery of training events. Trainers who operate from either stereotypical extreme are likely to switch off their participants.

Hofstede's work has had a major influence on learning and teaching in higher education where library staff and faculty may be working with groups of students from different cultural backgrounds. An understanding of these differences helps the trainer to be aware of the expectations of the students and their individual learning needs. Many colleges and universities provide introductory programs to these students to help them to understand the way the education system works and what they are likely to experience in this learning environment.

These ideas have also been applied in many education settings to the training of library and other support staff in responding to cultural diversity while providing different customer services such as help desks, circulation services and AV services.

WORKING WITH PEOPLE WITH SPECIAL NEEDS

Successful training events are inclusive, involve all the participants and provide a learning environment which is conducive to individual and group learning. People with disabilities sometimes have additional needs in order to enable them to fully participate in a course. The term "disabled people" includes a wide range of people with a wide range of additional needs which need to be taken into account when planning and delivering training sessions:

- people with physical disabilities
- people with learning disabilities
- people with mental health problems.

If you know that someone is coming on your training event who has additional needs then it is worthwhile contacting them and discussing these needs with them. This will enable you to be prepared and provide them with an excellent learning experience. If necessary gain additional support, for example by asking for a training assistant.

EXAMPLE

1   Varsha had broken her back five years previously. She walked with difficulty and was often in pain. The trainer asked her what he could do to support her on the forthcoming training event. She said she needed to stand up and walk around every ten minutes. She also said that she sometimes found it hard to concentrate. This information enabled the trainer to let Varsha know that it was OK to walk about during the session. The trainer also reassured Varsha that the course manual provided full course details – if she lost concentration at any time then she would be able to review the material at another time.

2   Linda was a newly appointed library assistant. She was very worried and panicky about attending the course. The trainer discussed her situation and discovered that Linda was dyslexic and was worried about having to write sentences or essays in public. The trainer reassured Linda that this wouldn't happen. The trainer then changed her course plan, for example one of the activities was changed from filling in a worksheet to completing a group mind map (this involved writing words and drawing symbols rather than writing sentences).

3   Suma had recently been in a traffic accident and had damaged his neck. It was in a neck brace. The trainer asked him what would help him to attend the course in comfort. Suma said a swivel chair and also being able to dress in casual clothes. This was then arranged.

4   Frances was a participant who was deaf and had a signer to help her on the training event. Before the event, the trainer met with Frances and her signer and discussed how they would like to work. As a result of this meeting, the trainer let all the participants and the signer have the course notes and OHP outlines in advance (this wasn't her normal practice). The trainer kept all the mini presentations to under ten minutes in length. She provided written guidelines to all the group activities (not her normal practice).

5   Victor's hearing was impaired and he was able to lip read. Before the training event the trainer asked Victor what would help him during the course. Victor's response was "wear lipstick, speak clearly, using no jargon and short sentences." The trainer, a woman, was easily able to respond to Victor's needs.

Checklist for working with people with special needs

(Adapted from B. Allan, *Running learning groups,* Folens, 1997).

PREPARING FOR THE STUDENTS

1 Have you identified any participants with special needs?
2 Have you met with them to discuss their additional needs and the approaches that you could take to support their learning and full participation?
3 Do you need to obtain additional support, e.g., through reading, signing or other special services?

PREPARING FOR THE COURSE

4 Have you identified an appropriate room with appropriate facilities?
5 Have you considered the additional needs of participants when preparing the course process, e.g., with regard to length of activity, type of activity, level and skills of student?
6 Have you reviewed your learning materials, e.g., for use of stereotypes in case studies and videos?
7 Have you considered the use of language in the course (both in the learning materials and what will you say yourself)?

RUNNING THE COURSE

8 In the introduction have you and the group established a set of common ground rules?
9 Has your language been inclusive?
10 Have you used a wide range of activities to enable everyone to participate?
11 Have you responded appropriately to discriminatory language or behavior?
12 Have you enabled people with additional needs to participate?
13 As the course has progressed, have you checked with the participants that their additional needs are being met?

GAINING SUPPORT

14 Have you identified additional sources of support to assist you in your work, e.g., colleagues, specialist staff within your organization, local support services, national support services?

Part 2

The training process

6
Linking training with the needs of the library

INTRODUCTION

> If you don't know where you are going then you won't know when you have got there.
>
> Anon

How is the training process linked with the needs (either current or future) of the library? The starting point is normally the overall training strategy which establishes the direction, priorities and training process. This is followed by detailed planning that takes place before a training event. One of the reasons for this detailed planning is to ensure that the training program meets the needs of the library. In this chapter, these themes are explored under the following headings:

- developing a training and staff development process in the library
- identifying training needs
- establishing training objectives.

DEVELOPING A TRAINING AND STAFF DEVELOPMENT PROCESS

A key ingredient in the training and development process is the recognition of staff development and training as a key library process. As such it is normally managed within the framework of an agreed policy. Hackett (1997) describes two main options for developing a training policy and these are shown in Table 6.1.

While staff training and development sometimes take place in an intuitive manner, to be effective they need to be an essential process. This normally involves gaining a commitment to staff training and development, from, for example, the chief executive, directors and senior managers. This commitment is then translated into a staff

training and development policy which is likely to contain the following elements:

- the aim of staff training and development within the library
- statement of who is responsible for staff training and development
- statement of who is eligible for training
- the process for identifying training needs
- types of training that are available and on what basis
- guidelines for access to training and development
- the balance between work-based learning and off-the-job training
- the forms of learning/learning outcomes that are preferred
- the process for applying and attending training
- the appeal process for decisions related to training.

Table 6.1   *Training policies (from P. Hackett, Introduction to training, IPD, 1997)*

Explicit	Intuitive
Based on careful analysis of organizational needs, best practice and law	Intuitive
Formally written down as a basis for future decisions	Inferred from the pattern of decisions previously made
Communicated to all employees to guide decision making	Referred to after the event to justify specific decisions
Prescriptive and all embracing	Allow considerable discretion
Supported by operating procedures	Unsupported
Part of an internally consistent framework, e.g., personnel policy, equal opportunities policy	Stand alone

An example staff training and development policy follows.

EXAMPLE

Sample Library Staff Development Policy

Staff development is an essential element in the development of the library. It should provide planned opportunities to support all staff in meeting the departmental objectives:

- to be the preferred provider of information services
- to provide a quality service
- to give value for money.

Staff development includes:

training which is sharply focused to cover specific skills or behaviors
development which is broader in focus and enables individuals to develop their knowledge and skills, and/or to experience personal development.

1   Aims and objectives

The prime aim of staff development is to support the current and future needs of the library. The objectives are to provide a planned and supported staff development process which will support:

- the achievement of the annual outcomes of the Department, teams and individuals
- the development of the Department to meet future requirements.

2   Access and entitlement

All library staff should expect:

- staff development opportunities to be available and to be consistent with the Equal Employment Opportunity Plan
- to participate in the staff development planning process through the performance management processes
- to disseminate to their colleagues the results of staff development undertaken
- to receive information and guidance on staff development opportunities
- support while undertaking staff development.

3   Staff development processes

Staff development involves a wide range of activities which enable an individual member of staff to develop his/her knowledge, skills or behavioral competencies. A list of typical activities is included in Appendix A. There are three main forms of staff development within the Department.

3.1 Orientation

An orientation program will be in place for all new members of library staff and this will be divided into activities during their first week of work and activities during their first six months in the Department. In their first month, all new library staff members will work through a training needs assessment with their line manager and this will result in an individual training plan.

New members of the staff will receive three levels of orientation in the Department:

First week
- introduction to team and other key members of staff
- introduction to relevant policies and procedures
- familiarization with key functions and tasks.

First six months
- introduction and appropriate experience in different areas of activity in the department
- introduction and guides to different sites and specialist working areas
- introduction and familiarization with relevant departments in the organization.

Special training activities
- planned training activities to enable new members of staff to carry out their work in an efficient and effective manner.

3.2 Staff development as a result of movement to a new role within the organization

In their first month, all new staff members will work through a training needs assessment with their line manager and this will result in an individual training plan. This will be implemented and supported by the line manager.

3.3 Performance management processes

These processes result in individual staff development plans which outline specific learning activities for members of staff. The responsibilities for implementing these plans are as follows:

Individual member of staff
- to seek out appropriate learning activities
- to request support for these activities

- to participate in these activities
- to disseminate their findings within their team and/or the Department.

Line managers

- to carry out the staff development planning process
- to support staff as they achieve their development plans
- to evaluate the outcomes of staff development activities
- to disseminate new ideas and initiatives within their teams and the Department.

Resources Manager

- to monitor and control the staff development processes
- to evaluate the staff development processes
- to disseminate new ideas and initiatives across the Department.

4   Departmental coordination of staff development

The Resources Manager has the responsibility for coordinating staff development activities through the staff development group. The staff development group is made up of staff representing all the teams, different sites and different levels of staff. The functions of this group are to:

- disseminate new ideas and approaches to staff development
- coordinate expenditure on staff development
- monitor and evaluate staff development activities.

5   Conflict of interests

In the event that a member of staff and their line manager are unable to reach agreement about particular staff development activities then the individual may approach the appropriate manager. In the event that this does not lead to a satisfactory outcome then the matter may be taken to the Resources Manager. If this proves unsatisfactory then the issue will be taken to the Director of the Library.

Appendix A   **Staff development activities**

Action learning

Coaching

Conferences

Courses

Demonstrations

Distance learning

Individual studies

Meetings

Mentoring

Open learning

Paired working

Project work

Research

Seminars

Short courses

Training courses

Visits

Work experience

Work shadowing

Writing reports or papers.

IDENTIFYING TRAINING NEEDS

The constantly changing internal and external environments in information and library services that are described in Chapter 1 result in a wide range of training needs. Training needs arise from three main types of activity within the library:

- implementing – bridging the gap between present and desired performance
- improving – improving performance to achieve continually rising standards
- innovating – doing new and better things.

Examples include: implementing new performance management processes such as appraisal programs, implementing a new IT or network system, improving performance through the introduction of new systems and procedures, or by developing and responding to new policies, e.g., customer service policies; or innovating through involvement in collaborative projects.

The development of a training plan or plans is an essential part of the training process and this plan will be aligned with the business plans of the library, with the objectives both of the whole department and of units and teams within it, and with the needs of individual staff.

The training plan is likely to identify the aim(s), rationale and link with library objectives, learning objectives/outcomes, skills and knowledge to be developed, training methods, numbers to be trained, duration of training, resource requirements and anticipated costs. One training plan may be developed for a whole library or a series of integrated training plans, which may be presented in terms of skills/knowledge to be developed or the groups of staff to be targeted.

ESTABLISHING TRAINING OBJECTIVES

There are a number of people whom it may be worthwhile consulting about training needs and they include:

- senior/top management
- middle managers and team leaders
- internal customers
- external customers

- intended participants themselves
- colleagues in other information and library services.

They will all be able to give a different perspective on the training needs of library staff. Hackett (1997) provides useful guidelines on this consultation process and identifies three principles to guide your choice:

- Consult until you are confident that there is a real need for the training and that you know what the need is.
- Consult the people who know most about the need.
- Consult the people who should be supporting the training and its outcomes, especially those who are disaffected or hostile.
- Hardingham (1996) provides the summary given in Table 6.2.

Table 6.2 *People to consult about training objectives* (Adapted from A. Hardingham, *Designing training*, IPD, 1996)

People	Pros	Cons
Customer (your key contact)	The person who pays the training bill! Their requirements need to be satisfied He/she may have very strong views and a high degree of clarity about what is to be achieved	He/she may have been asked to organize the training by someone else and may not be clear about what is to be achieved. If so, consult both him/her and the "real" customer
Senior/top management	They are likely to have a very good overview of what the organization's needs are If they support the training and its outcomes then it is very helpful and likely to improve training transfer	They may be too distant from the real issues driving the training You can't consult them about every single piece of training: you need to prioritize
Internal "customers" of participants	They may be very close to, and insightful about, the real training needs	Their view of what needs to change may be overinfluenced by their personal agendas
External customers of participants	This type of consultation can build strong relationships between the organization and its customers Training objectives will be directly linked to customer needs External people can add a unique and insightful perspective	Many participants do not have external customers It may be commercially risky to raise training needs with external customers Customers may simply not know enough about the issues
The participants themselves	This type of consultation can build commitment to the training before it starts Participants are closest of all to the issues	Participants may feel they are being "second-guessed" or manipulated Participants may feel that the trainers do not know what they are doing! Participants who are not consulted may feel disaffected

Whomever you consult, it is important to identify the specific aims, objectives and/or learning outcomes of the training event. It is worthwhile obtaining agreement in writing. This will then inform the planning, delivery and evaluation of the training event.

Learning outcomes

It is crucial to the success of the training program to identify its purpose and what will be achieved. This will enable you to plan an appropriate session and then evaluate it afterwards. There are a number of ways in which this can be expressed, either as aims, objectives or learning outcomes.

AIMS

These are a broad statement of what the program aims to achieve. The aims will answer questions such as:

- What is the purpose of this training event?
- What is the course intended to achieve?

OBJECTIVES

These are derived from the aims and they describe the specific intentions of the course. For example:

At the end of the course participants will be able to

- define customer service standards
- prepare an action plan.

They may be written at general or specific levels. For example:

general objective   Understand health and safety issues in the Learning Center

specific objective   Follow the correct procedures when hearing a fire alarm.

LEARNING OUTCOMES

This is another way of specifying what someone will gain from the course. A learning outcome specifies what the participants are likely to learn as a result of the training event. It is important to specify the learning outcomes accurately using words that describe evidence of the participant's learning. It is therefore helpful to avoid the use of words which describe non-observable states of mind. The following table gives examples of words to avoid and offers alternatives:

Table 6.3   *Language and learning outcomes* (Adapted from B. Allan and D. Lewis, *Program Planning Unit*, University of Lincolnshire and Humberside, 1999)

Avoid words like	Use words like
Know	State
Understand	Describe
Really know	Explain
Be familiar with	List
Become acquainted with	Evaluate
Have a good grasp of	Identify
Appreciate	Distinguish between
Be interested in	Analyze
Acquire a feel for	Outline
Be aware of	Summarize
Believe	Represent graphically
Have information about	Apply
Realize the significance of	Assess
Learn the basics of	Give examples of
Obtain a working knowledge of	Suggest reasons why

Learning outcomes are best written in straightforward language, e.g.,

- Explain and evaluate the role of . . .
- Describe and apply the principles of . . .
- Investigate the effectiveness of . . .
- Design and implement . . .
- Research the field of . . .
- Implement a new system to . . .
- Deliver a presentation to . . .

In order to achieve each learning outcome it is likely that a range of actions will need to be undertaken.

Examples of aims, objectives and learning outcomes are provided below. In addition, many of the sample programs presented throughout the book contain examples too.

EXAMPLE

This example demonstrates the use of an aim and objectives.

Example training event outline	
Title	Using e-mail
Aim	To introduce participants to e-mail.
Objectives	By the end of the training event, participants will have:
	• sent and received e-mail
	• practiced using the address book and distribution list

	• practiced subscribing to e-mail lists
	• practiced accessing news groups.
Learning methods	Mini presentation(s), practical hands-on activities, learning manual
Audience	All library staff
Pre-course requirements	Able to log in to college system. Able to use a mouse.
Trainer	Jane Smith
Date	06/09/99
Venue	Room 129, Main library building

EXAMPLE

Another example that shows an aim and objectives.

Example training event outline	
Title	Customer as learner workshop
Aim	The aim of the workshop is to enable Learning Support staff to develop their understanding of their role in helping students to become independent learners.
Objectives	By the end of the training event, participants will have: • defined customer service models in Learning Support • recognized the need for a commitment to independent learning • examined their own approaches to learning • identified how Learning Support supports independent learning • identified how learning styles have an impact on the customer interface • considered factors in Learning Support that have a positive or negative effect on student learning.
Learning methods	Mini presentation(s), group activities, use of questionnaires, whole group discussion.
Audience	All Learning Support staff
Precourse requirements	None
Trainer	D. Smith
Date	02/16/99
Venue	Room 129, Main Learning Support building

EXAMPLE

This example shows the use of learning outcomes.

REPORT WRITING

Program outline

This workshop provides a range of practical techniques and the opportunity to practice them:

• identifying the purpose of the report

- identifying the reader and their needs
- structuring the report
- writing the report
- using persuasive writing techniques
- improving the first and subsequent drafts
- editing and completing the report
- presenting the report.

Why you should attend

Busy library staff are often asked to write reports. This course offers a practical guide to the report writing process. It is relevant to all library staff who are involved in report writing – either short or long reports, technical or less technical reports. It will help you to write well structured, readable and persuasive reports. It will help you to get to grips with the report writing process so that you are able to work quickly and effectively to produce an excellent report.

Learning methods

The course is a very practical, participative event. It includes mini presentations, individual and small group activities and exercises. All participants receive a course manual.

Learning outcomes

On completing the course, participants will be able to:

- write a report for a specific purpose and a specific audience
- structure the report in a logical manner
- identify and use their own report writing strategy
- use a series of persuasive writing techniques
- edit and improve their initial draft
- select and use an appropriate presentation format.

7

Designing effective training programs

INTRODUCTION

This chapter is concerned with designing effective training programs and learning environments. The ideas in this chapter can be applied to the design of individual or group sessions. The following topics are covered:

- using the 4MAT approach
- ten fundamental design principles.

Why design your training sessions? The benefits of planning your training session include:

- it gives you confidence so that you won't dry up
- it focuses your thinking on the needs of the learner
- it helps you to be prepared with appropriate learning materials
- it helps you to anticipate possible problems and develop contingency plans
- it enables you to think through the whole event and take into account the principles of effective learning
- you are less likely to make basic errors during the training event
- it looks professional.

The design process enables you to work out the learning process in detail, i.e., the structure, content and sequence of all the activities that will enable you to meet the aim and objectives/outcomes of the training event. The result of the design process is a detailed training plan and this is likely to contain the following:

- title
- name of trainer

- session aims/objectives/learning outcomes
- content
- delivery methods
- learning materials and visual aids
- timetable for the event with the timing of each activity
- outline of each activity
- details of the evaluation process.

There is no simple solution to or prescription for designing effective training programs. Success depends on the following factors:

- organizational and individual learning needs (see Chapters 5 and 6)
- setting realistic objectives that win participants' commitment (see Chapter 5)
- incorporating key learning principles (see Chapter 2)
- incorporating key design principles (covered in this chapter)
- accommodating individual differences (see Chapter 2 and this chapter)
- using an appropriate physical environment (covered in this chapter and also Chapter 2)
- using a trainer who is knowledgeable, skilled and committed to make the training event work (see Chapters 3 and 4).

Successful training event design involves the integration and balancing of these different factors. The focus in this chapter is on design principles and this is approached from two different perspectives:

- a standard format for organizing and ordering a training session (the 4MAT approach)
- identifying fundamental design principles.

THE 4MAT APPROACH

The 4MAT approach to designing either a whole training event or a particular training activity, e.g., presentation, is based on the work of Kolb (1985) and Honey and Mumford (see pp. 23–30). In this approach the training activity/session is divided into four distinct areas: why, what, how, what if; in addition there is a start that includes opening the training event and stating what it is about (little what) and also a close.

This approach to planning training programs/activities using learning styles offers a very clear guide to planning learning programs. Basically, each session needs to be planned in the following order:

- **Open training event.** This includes the welcome. Introduction to the course. Introduction to each other with a possible icebreaker. Housekeeping arrangements.

- **Little what.** This lets people know what the training event is about. This may take one or two minutes.
- **Why.** The trainer explains the rationale and benefits of the training event. This will appeal to the reflectors in the group whose mind will be focused on "Why are we doing this?" Once this question is answered, reflectors are able to move on to other stages in the learning cycle.
- **What.** This is concerned with providing the detail. Theorists, in particular, love this stage of a learning event. If they are not kept in check then they will ask many "what" questions which could prevent the trainer from moving on to the next stage. This is particularly true if the trainer's preferred learning style is that of theorist too.
- **How.** This is the hands-on activities part of the session. Participants are able to gain experience of how the key ideas, processes or systems work in practice. They are also able to exchange their practical experiences with others. This is the part that appeals to activists.
- **What if.** This part of a training event is often managed as a series of questions from the participants with an open discussion. This enables them to relate their learning to future workplace situations.
- **Closure.** This involves closing the training session. Ensuring that all activities, etc., are completed. Evaluation. Farewells.

EXAMPLE

An example program that demonstrates the 4MAT training method. This example was first presented in Chapter 2, p. 26. It is amended here to show the 4MAT approach.

Title: Learning styles at work in a college library

Background: This half-day training session was designed for a team of 17 college library, IT and media support staff. It was led by an external facilitator.

Learning objectives: By the end of the session, staff will be able to:

- describe the four different learning styles
- identify their own preferred learning style
- identify the preferred learning styles of individual students
- respond to students according to individual learning styles.

Outline program

	Activity	Resources	4MAT approach
	Music as people arrive. Mozart and/or Verdi.	Music – CDs and player	
1	Introductions – everyone to say their name and what they want from the session. Housekeeping arrangements.	Introduction	
2	Very brief introduction to learning styles.	Flipchart paper	Little what
3	Activity: why is it important to know and use ideas about learning styles. Small group activity – groups of two/three. Each group to come up with up to five reasons. Debrief. Flipchart findings.	Flipchart paper	Why

	Activity	Resources	4MAT approach
4	Learning styles inventory – introduce inventory. Ask everyone to complete inventory. As people finish it then suggest they share their findings with their neighbor.	Inventory Pencils	What
5	Debrief learning styles inventory exercise. Discuss process. Discuss findings. Give a "health and safety" warning re: labelling/ stereotyping		What
6	Break	Tea/coffee/ bagels Music – CDs and player	
7	Welcome back. Quick review of four learning styles. Ask people to move into groups according to learning styles, i.e., all activists together, pragmatists, etc. If more than six people with same learning style then split them into two groups. Ask them to identify their likes and dislikes with regard to learning. Ask them to write these on flipchart paper. Ask them to share their findings. Trainer may also include observations re: exercise process, e.g., activists are likely to complete it first, theorists are likely to want to discuss in detail.	Flipchart paper Pens	Mini review of What How
8	Brief input – how individuals ask questions arising from their learning style preference: theorists – why, reflectors – what, activists – how, pragmatists – what if. Discuss relevance to working on a help desk or leading an information skills session	Flipchart paper and pens	How
9	Activity – what will you do in practice as a result of these new ideas? Ask them to work in groups of people with different learning styles (try and get one of each in each group). Ask them to develop a list of practical strategies for their work. These need to be written on flipchart paper. Share their findings with the whole group.	Flipchart paper and pens	What if
10	Action planning. Ask everyone to identify one thing that they will do as a result of today's session. Ask them to share it with the whole group.		What if
11	Evaluate the session	Standard form	End
12	End the session. Thank the participants.		End

EXAMPLE

An example program that demonstrates the 4MAT training method. This example was first presented in Chapter 2, p. 39. It is amended here to show the 4MAT approach.

Title: Team building for the future

Background: This event was designed and led by an external trainer. It was provided for a group of eight information staff working in a legal services organization.

Aims: The aim of this event is to improve team working within the library.

Learning objectives: By the end of the event, team members will have:

* identified the characteristics of an excellent team
* assessed their own team strengths and areas of development
* explored a model of effective teamwork
* developed a team action plan
* developed individual action plans.

Resources: flowers; flipchart, paper and pens; teamwork inventory; range of CDs and player.

Time	Activity	4MAT approaches
	Prepare room. Welcome sign – flipchart. Flowers. Music. Coffee/tea on arrival.	
9:15	Introductions. Housekeeping.	Introduction
9:30	General introduction to the course. Objectives. Participants work in pairs. What I want to get out of the day (5 minutes). Flipchart findings.	Little what Why
9:45	Characteristics of an effective team. Brainstorm. Write on flipchart.	What
10:00	Introduction to teamwork theory and framework. Team building activity Music in background.	What How
11:00	Break with refreshments. Put on music.	
11:15	Debrief activity.	How
12:00	Teamwork inventory. Complete questionnaire. Music.	How
12:30	Discussion. Any questions. End morning session.	How
12:30– 1:15	Lunch	
1:15	Video on teamwork. Participants complete questionnaire using information from video. Hand out mints. Discussion.	How
2:15	Implications for team leaders. Discussion. Flipchart key points.	What if?
2:45	Implications for team members. Pairs exercise. Use worksheet.	What if?
3:15	Break with refreshments. Put on music.	
3:30	Team action planning session – group exercise carried out standing up. Flipchart top ten actions.	What if?
4:00	Individual action planning – pairs exercise.	What if?
4:20	Course evaluation.	Close
4:30	End	Close

TEN FUNDAMENTAL DESIGN PRINCIPLES

Hardingham (1996) has described ten fundamental design principles that will enable the trainer to:

* establish credibility
* obtain the participants' commitment
* manage risk
* attract attention
* be flexible.

These are set out in Table 7.1.

Table 7.1 *Ten fundamental design principles* (From A. Hardingham, *Designing training*, IPD, 1996)

Design principles	Key concepts				
	Credibility	Commitment	Risk	Attention	Flexibility
1 Maximize action and interaction		+	+	+	
2 Signpost, signpost, and then signpost again	+	+	+	+	
3 Vary pace and rhythm				+	
4 Chunk content				+	+
5 Map the participants' world	+	+		+	
6 Give participants choices		+	+		+
7 Surface objections		+	+	+	+
8 Balance theory and practice	+			+	
9 Design in feedback		+	+		
10 Design for closure		+		+	

1 Maximize action and interaction

This is a key point and involves designing *all* elements of a training program to involve the participants in action and interaction either individually, in small groups or as a whole group. Presentations may become interactive by including question and answer sessions. The more the participants are involved in the session then the more likely they are to benefit from it. Action and interaction enhance learning as is shown in Figure 7.1. An extensive range of different training activities is presented in Chapter 9.

Listening only 5%

Reading 10%

Audiovisual 20%

Demonstration 30%

Discussion group 50%

Practice by doing 75%

Teach others or immediate use 90%

Figure 7.1 *Average retention rates*

2 Signpost

As the trainer you will know in detail what is going to happen in your training event and the design rationale behind it. The participants do not have this information. Some participants may not even know why they are attending the training event. It is therefore really important to signpost and guide the participants through the event. Signposting means letting the participants know:

- the structure of the day
- training methods and techniques
- housekeeping arrangements
- why they are doing what they are doing, i.e., the rationale behind each activity
- what is expected of them, i.e., what they are going to be asked to do
- how they will be working (individually, in pairs, in small groups, as a whole group)
- your expectations, e.g., use of questions, what to do if they don't understand.

One of the results of signposting is that participants feel safe and comfortable within their learning environment. This will help enhance their learning. A lack of signposting may cause some participants to become confused, angry or irritated.

3 Vary pace and rhythm

A training event is an experience – a little like a play, TV drama, football match or piece of music. Varying the pace and rhythm will help to enhance the impact of the event.

Slow pace activities include the following:

- small group discussions
- reading
- completing questionnaires
- storytelling
- watching a video
- practicing a new skill.

Fast pace activities include:

- high energy mini presentations
- jokes and humor
- fast-paced question and answer sessions
- quizzes
- many games
- activities carried out under a tight time schedule.

When you are planning your training session you need to think about creating variety in pace and rhythm. You may want to create a wave-like effect by mixing and matching different types of activities. You may want to create surprises so that the participant is relaxed at one stage and then out of breath at another. Do you want to go with the energy of a group, for example, by including a quiet activity during the famous after lunch lull or do you want to change the energy at this point into something more upbeat and exciting?

4 Chunk content

Chunking involves breaking down the content of your training and presenting it in manageable chunks. Typically people's attention may wane in the middle of an activity rather than at the beginning or end of it. By building in lots of beginnings and endings you build in many more learning points to your training session.

EXAMPLE

A training program for library staff on evaluating Internet sources may be chunked in the following way:

1	Introductions – name and what you want to obtain from the session (10 minutes)
2	Reasons for evaluating Internet sources (Input – 10 minutes)
3	Criteria for evaluating Internet sources (Checklist – 10 minutes)
4	Best and worst sites! (Practical hands-on session – 30 minutes)
5	Any questions? (Open forum – 10 minutes)
6	BREAK
7	Even more sites! (Online quiz – 30 minutes)
8	Summary of key lessons learned (15 minutes)
9	Handout – useful websites (5 minutes)
10	Points to beware of when supporting student learning (10 minutes)
11	Individual action planning session (5 minutes)
12	Evaluation of session (5 minutes)
13	End session

Breaking down the session in this way enables the participants to see how the topics are going to be covered and also the order of events. They can see the variety that is built into the program and know how the time is allocated.

The trainer can also use this program to obtain more flexibility. For example, questions raised in chunk 5 may need to be answered by changing the program slightly. Participants who need to see the relevance to their job may need to have chunk 10 moved earlier in the program.

5 Map the participants' world

This involves moulding the program so that it fits into the world of the participants. This means:

- using the same type of language as the participants
- using examples from their world

- starting off at their speed, e.g., by matching breathing patterns, and then moving forward
- acknowledging current events and situations.

This helps to create rapport and ensures that the participants engage in the program and find it credible and valuable to their particular situation.

EXAMPLE

At a recent conference I saw a presenter who made a series of key blunders which ensured that he did not map the participants' world (they were all school library staff). He gave a 30-minute presentation which started off a morning's training session. He used a large number of acronyms that very few people understood and his examples were from academic libraries rather than school libraries. He started off at a gallop before people had an opportunity to settle down and "get their bearings" and, the final insult, his PowerPoint presentation had been prepared for a presentation to a group of college lecturers and included many irrelevant examples. The presenter's main message was rejected and the school librarians did not engage in what he had to say. The result of his behavior was a very angry and irritated audience and very little learning taking place.

6 Give the participants choices

The majority of learners are likely to feel more comfortable and in control of their own learning processes if they are given choices during the training event. You will increase their commitment to the training event if they feel they are being treated with respect and as adults. Hardingham (1996) describes the following kinds of possible choices:

- whether to work alone, in pairs, or in groups
- whether to ask for feedback from the trainer
- whether to volunteer to do something in front of the group
- whether to share information or work in private
- with whom in the group to work.

Other choices include:

- what role to take in different exercises
- where to work during group activities, e.g., in training room, outside, foyer, café
- when to have breaks or lunch (if there is a choice over these factors).

7 Surface objections

Sometimes people arrive at training events with criticisms or objections to one or more aspects of the planned activities. If they do not have an opportunity to voice these then they are unlikely to engage in the learning process. Similarly, they may develop criticisms as the event progresses.

Building in time to bring out these objections or criticisms is useful as it means they can be dealt with and, it is hoped, the participant will then become engaged in the learning process.

Just before the start of a training event for a group of library staff one of the participants said to the trainer "I don't know what the purpose of this session is. I haven't had a chance to say what I want to happen today." As part of the introductory session, the trainer asked all the participants what they wanted from the day's session. Their responses were written up on a flipchart. The event was then tailored to meet their needs. This satisfied everyone.

8 Balance theory and practice

According to Hardingham (1996), "Participants generally expect some kind of theoretical underpinning to training. You will lose credibility if it is totally skills and practice. Too much theory switches people off, though." So, you need to create a balance between theory and practice. On a six-hour training course perhaps one or two fifteen-minute theoretical inputs are sufficient.

If you are a trainer whose preferred learning style is theorist then you may be tempted to present too much theory and/or you may be diverted by interesting theoretical questions or issues. Conversely, activists may be tempted to skimp on the theory and move into activities and exercises too soon. As a trainer you need to develop a balance so that everyone is satisfied. Providing a detailed reading list will help to satisfy the information needs of the theorists.

9 Design in feedback

Feedback is an essential part of the learning process. High quality feedback enhances learning and will also increase the motivation of the learner. It also helps to focus attention. Feedback needs to be built into the training event.

Feedback may be given by the trainer and/or the participants. It is very important that whoever gives the feedback follows the basic rules. These are described in Chapter 4.

10 Design for closure

Well designed training programs have a clear beginning, middle and end. The trainer needs to signal that the event is moving toward closure. Then the actual ending needs to promote a sense of achievement, completion and closure. Different approaches to closing a training event are covered in Chapter 9.

8
Preparing the learning environment

INTRODUCTION

Few libraries employ special staff to be responsible for staff development, and administrative support is often at a premium. This means that many library trainers manage all the practical aspects of running a training event, including administration activities, venue and training room arrangements, and also create the learning environment. A lone library trainer may do everything from sending out letters to participants providing them with details of the training event through moving the furniture.

The aim of this chapter is to provide guidance on the factors that need to be taken into account when planning and setting up the learning environment. It covers the following themes:

- training administration
- the learning environment
- learning resources
- providing a safe environment
- the trainer's kit.

TRAINING ADMINISTRATION

This section of the book presents a series of checklists for trainers to use when they are planning their events. It includes:

- course planning checklist
- registration checklist
- venue evaluation checklist.

Course planning checklist

COURSE MANAGEMENT TEAM

1 Team coordinator
2 Team members
3 Responsibility for course planning and delivery
4 Responsibility for venue and learning resources
5 Responsibility for course administration
6 Responsibility for course review and evaluation

COURSE OUTLINE

7 Aims, objectives and learning outcomes
8 Title
9 Duration of course and sessions
10 Outline program
11 Trainer – skills, experience, style, possible names
12 Participants – number, background and experience, prerequisites
13 Preferred dates

VENUE OUTLINE

14 Preferred venue, location, type of accommodation
15 Number and style of rooms required
16 Residential/nonresidential
17 Meals and refreshment times
18 Funds available

LEARNING MATERIALS AND RESOURCES

19 Names and bibliographical details of trainer(s)
20 Printed materials
   – Handouts
   – Manuals
   – Textbook(s)
21 AV materials
   – Videos
   – Video player
   – Whiteboard
   – Flipchart
   – OHP and screen
22 IT requirements
   – Computer equipment
   – Videoconferencing equipment
   – ISDN line

23 Other
  – Special stationery, folders, pens, etc.

ORGANIZATIONAL REQUIREMENTS

24 Travel arrangements
  – Negotiated special rates
  – Transport of participants
25 Responsibility/authority
  – For preliminary arrangements
  – For confirming arrangements
  – On course
26 Payment of fees
27 Payment of expenses
28 Are security passes needed?
29 Insurance

Registration checklist

COVER LETTER

1 Welcome
2 Name of participant and organization or department
3 Course title
4 Date and day
5 Venue and time to arrive
6 Refreshment arrangements
7 Special amenities
8 Dietary options
9 Access facilities

PROGRAM DETAILS

10 Program outline
11 Course aims, objectives and learning outcomes
12 Precourse work

TRAVEL ARRANGEMENTS

13 Map
14 Car parking
  – Parking permit
15 Public transport – bus, rail, air
16 Taxi phone numbers

ADDITIONAL INFORMATION

    17 List of participants
    18 Precourse questionnaire
    19 Venue brochure
    20 Expenses claim form
    21 Confirmation slip
    22 Cancellation clause
    23 Visits or trips
    24 Name badges

RESIDENTIAL

    25 Type of room
    26 Meal times
    27 Mail/message arrangements
    28 Telephone/fax/e-mail numbers
    29 Dietary options
    30 Access facilities
    31 How the bill will be paid
        – Accommodation
        – Food
        – Drinks
    32 Recreation facilities
        – Sport
        – Food and drink
        – Visits or trips
        – Other
    33 Evening work expectations.

Venue evaluation checklist

(Adapted from M. Saunders and K. Holdaway, *The lone trainer*, Kogan Page, 1993)

    1 Location
        – Town
        – Country
    2 Type of venue
        – Hotel
        – University/college
        – Conference center
        – Other
    3 Environment
        – Quiet
        – Business-like buzz.

4   Ease of access
    – by car
    – by train
    – by bus
    – from airport
    – for people with additional needs, e.g., wheelchair users
5   Parking
6   Convenience for
    – Outside visits
    – Downtown
    – Shops, post office, bank
    – Sports facilities
    – Countryside
    – Religious institutions
7   Access to grounds for outside exercises
8   Reputation
9   Star rating
10 Trainer's preferences
11 Opinions of other users
12 Costs

THE LEARNING ENVIRONMENT

The nature of the learning environment will depend on the aims and objectives of the training program, the size of the group and the trainer's preferences. The following checklist can be used to help identify the facilities required in a training room.

Nature of training rooms

(Adapted from M. Saunders and K. Holdaway, *The lone trainer,* Kogan Page, 1993)

ROOMS

1   Number of rooms available
2   Access to small group rooms
3   Size – length, width, height
4   Shape and sight lines (including pillars)
5   Seating arrangement
    – Theater style
    – Circle of chairs
    – "U" shaped with tables
    – Boardroom style
    – Cafe style
6   Type of chairs and tables
7   Availability of alternative chairs, e.g., for people with health problems

8   Access for people with disabilities
9   Access to an induction loop
10   Availability of water jugs/glasses/hard candies
11   Separate space for refreshments and lunch
12   Convenient restrooms
13   Place to hang coats and store luggage

RESOURCES FOR TRAINING EVENTS

14   Platform/stage/dais
15   Lectern or arrangements for speakers
16   Public address system
17   Screen for OHP
18   Whiteboard
19   Flipchart
20   Display space, e.g., for completed flipchart sheets
21   Projection facilities
22   Facilities for videotaping/tape recording event
23   Power points (number and voltage)
24   Access to ISDN
25   Access to videoconferencing
26   Access for other equipment

ENVIRONMENT

27   Heating and ventilation (who controls it, is it noisy?)
28   Air-conditioning (noise, windchill)
29   Lighting
      – Daylight
      – Dimming facilities
      – Curtains/blinds/blackout
30   Décor (unobtrusive)
31   Presence of large fixed mirrors (can be distracting)

SUPPORT SERVICES

32   Access to services
      – translation services
      – reprographic facilities
      – fax
33   Servicing of room(s)
      – Cleanliness
      – Replenishment of drinks/snacks, etc.
34   Access to room(s)
      – Time to set up
      – Locking of room(s) during breaks/overnight

35 Access to staff
– Audiovisual technician
– IT technician
– Catering staff

Furniture arrangements

There are many different types of furniture arrangements and these are summarized in Table 8.1 below.

Table 8.1 *Summary of different types of seating arrangements*

Arrangement	Uses	Advantages	Disadvantages
Theater style	Talks and seminars to large groups, e.g., over 20 participants. Regularly used for keynote presentations at conferences.	An efficient seating arrangement that enables large numbers to be seated. Presenter is clearly "in control." Visual aids easy to use.	Very formal arrangement. May intimidate some people (including the speaker). More difficult to build up rapport and interaction.
Horseshoe style (using tables and chairs)	Good for experiential activities and discussions.	Promotes discussion and interaction. Helps the group to form an identity. Relatively informal and allows the trainer to move into the horseshoe space and have one-to-one conversations. Facilitates the use of visual aids, handouts, etc.	Only works for a relatively small group – up to 16 participants.
Horseshoe style (using only chairs)	Seminars, workshops, discussions.	Promotes discussion and interaction. Helps the group to form an identity. Relatively informal and allows the trainer to move into the horseshoe space and have one-to-one conversations. Easy to move into smaller groups.	Some people may feel intimidated if they don't have a table in front of them.
Board style (everyone sits around a large table)	Often used in formal meetings.	Sets a formal tone. Everyone can see everyone else. Interaction is relatively easy.	Can intimidate and restrict interactions. It is not always easy for the trainer to move freely around the group.
Classroom style (rows of tables and chairs)	Sometimes used in workshops and skill training sessions.	Useful for accommodating large numbers.	Can foster "back to school" feelings. Does not encourage interaction or participation.
Restaurant or "bistro" style (small groups cluster around individual tables)	Useful for workshops and seminars. Increasingly used at conferences for keynote presentations, seminars, discussions.	Easy to interact with a small group. Promotes group work and discussion. Trainer(s) can move between groups easily.	There is a danger that cliques form. People with special needs, e.g., people with hearing impairment, may find it difficult to follow others' speech (as people are not always facing each other).

Improving the learning environment

Frequently, in library training situations we have little control over the choice of the venue and/or training room(s). Often library trainers are faced with a training scenario that does not match the ideal. The task is then to transform the room into something more appropriate. This may be achieved through the following:

- reorganizing furniture
- use of posters on walls
- use of flowers
- use of aromatherapy
- use of music.

EXAMPLE

In one college library, the author met a librarian who ran orientation programs. She worked in a "training room" that was also the room where unwanted furniture awaited disposal. The trainer used to bring a few cotton bedspreads from home. She would drape these across piles of unwanted furniture in the "training room." This immediately improved the appearance as well as giving a strong message to the course participants that she cared about them.

LEARNING RESOURCES

Effective learning resources help the learner(s) to meet their learning outcomes. A vast range of learning materials are used in library training sessions and they include:

- generic off-the-shelf general training materials
- generic off-the-shelf open learning materials
- customized general training materials
- customized open learning materials.

Training materials range from multimedia learning packages containing interactive CD-ROMS and associated printed materials to printed hand-outs prepared and distributed by individual trainers. Remember to make sure that you are not infringing copyright law when you prepare training materials.

A checklist of criteria to be met when quality learning resources are developed or purchased is given below. This checklist is adapted from J. Gough, *Developing learning materials*, IPD, 1996.

Checklist of quality criteria for learning resources

AIMS AND OBJECTIVES

- The learning materials support the learner(s) in meeting the objective(s) of the session.

CONTENT

- Clear instructions on how to use the materials
- Relevant and up-to-date
- Tells you where to get information
- The subject matter specified in the objective(s) is covered in detail
- Good supporting information
- Provides examples that represent a culturally diverse society.

STRUCTURE AND ORGANIZATION

- Clearly defined
- Logical sequence
- Can be updated
- Can be customized.

LEARNER CONTROL

- Easy to use
- Can be used in different ways.

EXERCISES AND ACTIVITIES

- Clear instructions on how to complete activity
- Allows for a mix of views and answers
- Starts with simple questions, then builds toward more complex activities
- Allows for reviewing/positive feedback by trainer/facilitator, or builds this into the material itself
- Interactive
- User-friendly
- Enjoyable.

APPEARANCE

- Attractive – use of boxes, shading, typeface, symbols, bullet points, etc.
- Self-explanatory

- Consistent presentation
- Good use of color, highlighting, graphics, illustrations
- Appropriate typographic style and size
- Printed material is well spaced
- Text is split into manageable chunks
- Clear headings and subheadings.

LANGUAGE

- Aimed at the right level
- Easy to understand
- Friendly and informal tone
- Inclusive
- Technical terms and jargon explained.

SUPPORT

- Adequate support provided, e.g., by trainer.

Obtaining learning resources

A wide range of learning resources is available and their advantages and limitations are described in Chapter 9 under the heading Audiovisual aids. Alternatively, relatively simple and attractive printed learning resources are easy to design and develop using standard word processing and desktop publishing packages. Figures 8.1 and 8.2 show some examples.

PROVIDING A SAFE ENVIRONMENT

All trainers have a responsibility for health and safety issues during their training programs. This is likely to involve them in:

- understanding the health and safety policy of their organization
- carrying out a risk assessment on the training room(s)
- explaining key health and safety information to course participants
- taking responsibility for explaining safety procedures to course participants
- following safe working procedures personally
- making sure that protective clothes and equipment are used when necessary
- encouraging safety participation and hazard reporting by learners
- reporting any accidents or near misses to the appropriate person.

Using a colorful approach

Are your sessions **colorful**?

Do you use **multisensory** approaches to learning?

Do your sessions **enliven** students?

Do they come out of them **energized?**

Do you use all the **senses?**

Hearing   e.g., background music on arrival and during activities

Smell   e.g., aromatherapy

Taste   e.g., unusual candies, cookies, high quality tea and coffee

Touch   e.g., in games and exercises

Sight   e.g., colored pens and paper
colorful name badges
flowers and plants
pictures which stimulate and relax.

Figure 8.1   *Handout for in-house training skills session for academic librarians* (Adapted from C. Beel et al., *Successful strategies: A handbook for trainers and educators,* CCDU, 1995)

Note: Words printed in bold were in color on handout.

Are you lonely?
Work on your own?
Hate making decisions?

Then hold a meeting

You get to see other people.
Offload decisions. Feel important
and impress your colleagues.

And all during work time!

Meetings

↓

"The practical alternative to work"

Figure 8.2   *Handout to start a training event on effective meetings*

If you are a trainer running an event in unfamiliar surroundings then it is important that you check the following *before* the program starts:

- emergency exits
- emergency procedure, e.g., in the case of fire
- emergency assembly points
- access to a telephone (if you need to make a 911 phone call)
- the training room(s) – that they provide a safe learning environment
- training equipment, e.g., computers.

In addition, if you are an independent trainer then it is worthwhile checking that you are covered by appropriate insurance.

EXAMPLE

An assistant librarian in a university library was running an introduction to the Internet course for new students. The venue was an IT laboratory on the ground floor. She had been informed in advance that one of the participants was in a wheelchair. At the start of the session, as part of the introductions, she went through the emergency procedures and made sure that everyone had stored their bags, etc., under the work benches to provide a clear exit route. Halfway through the session the fire alarm went off. She gave clear instructions to the group to evacuate the building and asked one of the students to push the person in the wheelchair. Everyone did as she requested and they evacuated the building in less than 60 seconds.

THE TRAINER'S KIT

What do trainers need when they are running training programs? The following checklist was compiled by asking a number of different library trainers what they like to take with them for training events.

30-plus useful items

1 Blutack
2 Post-it notes
3 3 × 5 index cards
4 colored paper
5 24 multicolored felt tip pens
6 box of new pencils
7 pencil sharpener
8 ballpoint pens
9 calculator
10 whiteboard markers
11 flipchart paper markers
12 blank OHP transparencies

13 OHP transparency nonpermanent pens
14 paper clips
15 blank flipchart paper
16 travel clock
17 cooking timer
18 tissues
19 paper towels
20 stapler
21 2-hole puncher
22 4-hole puncher
23 pair of scissors
24 packet of mints or stick of gum
25 plastic bag
26 sticky labels
27 electrical adaptor/distributor plug
28 extension cord
29 name tags
30 needle and thread
31 extra paper – white and colored
32 flashlight
33 CD/tape player
34 assortment of CDs and audiotapes
35 large plastic container to keep it all in!

9
Training methods

INTRODUCTION

There is a wide variety of training methods and techniques that a trainer can use. This chapter presents a range of them in alphabetical order:

- action planning
- audiovisual aids
- brainstorming
- buzz groups
- case studies
- debates
- demonstrations
- discussions
- games
- learning contracts
- lectures
- mind mapping
- packaged learning programs
- practical exercises
- presentations
- question and answer session
- questionnaires
- questions
- role play
- simulation
- small groups
- snowballing
- stories and metaphors.

Individual trainers should follow the guidance and ideas given in Chapter 7 to help them select the methods appropriate to their needs.

ACTION PLANNING

All trainers need to be aware of the importance of action plans both for themselves in terms of planning and delivering a successful training session and also as a learning tool. Action plans may be used at a number of different stages in the training process:

- before training starts as individuals write action plans that identify their learning goals, outcomes and subsequent actions – this may take place as part of a performance management process
- during training, e.g., as a learning contract with the trainer
- at the end of the training process, e.g., to enable course participants to transfer their learning into the workplace
- after training, e.g., with their manager and team leader when they negotiate and decide their next learning activity.

Research (e.g., by Goleman, 1996) suggests that people who develop and write down personal action plans are more likely to be successful than those who do not. A personal action plan can assist the participants to focus on areas requiring work and set achievable targets for improvement.

The key to a good action plan is that it should be SMART:

- **S**pecific, i.e., an identifiable action
- **M**easurable, i.e., there is something to see or hear that will show that the action has taken place
- **A**chievable, i.e., be manageable within the working environment of the library
- **R**ealistic, i.e., the participant will realistically be able to achieve it
- **T**imebound, i.e., a deadline is set or time allocated on a regular basis.

Example action plan forms are presented in Figures 9.1 and 9.2.

EXAMPLE

This exercise provides a useful way of introducing SMART objectives and it also provides an icebreaker and energizer. You will need a watch or clock with a seconds hand and at least one juggling ball.

Set up

Explain to the group that you are going to demonstrate working with objectives. Ask for five volunteers and ask them to come and stand at the front/center of the room. Say that all they will be asked to do is pass a ball from one person to the next.

Part I

Give them a juggling ball and ask them to pass the ball around all five people as quickly as possible. There are two rules: everyone must touch the ball and it must end up with the person who starts with the ball; only one person can touch the ball at a time. Let them practice a few times and then time them. They are likely to achieve the goal in three to ten seconds.

Part 2

Next ask them to repeat the exercise and this time set a challenging time limit, e.g., less than one second. Let them work out how to do it. Then time them achieving this goal. Finally, thank the volunteers, give them a round of applause and ask them to sit down.

Debriefing

Next process the results of the exercise. What happens (normally) in this exercise is that in Part 1 the volunteers achieve the goal and in Part 2 they achieve the SMART objective. The effect of the SMART objective is that it increases motivation, creativity and humor. In Part 2 the participants who have not volunteered often do things such as shout instructions, etc., which demonstrates that they have become involved too. One of the effects of this exercise is that it provides a powerful internal image of the impact of using SMART objectives.

Exercise variation

In Part 2 ask everyone in the group to get into groups of five and follow Part 2 instructions. If there are people who are left out then ask them to be timekeepers and monitors.

A personal action plan

Now that you have completed the training session decide on your immediate priority for action. Completing the questions below will help you plan for it effectively.

1 What will you do as a result of the training event?
Choose a starting point. Choose a very specific activity or task. Be realistic and choose something that you know you will do.

2 What resources will you need to do your activity?
Do you need any special books? Do you need access to a computer? Do you need any equipment?

3 What support will you need?
Will it be easier if you do it with a colleague? Perhaps you will need help from someone else?

4 When will you have completed your task OR how often will you do it?
Set a specific date and time OR set yourself a target, e.g., 15 minutes every day.

5 Who will check your progress and review your activity with you?
Get a colleague to ask how you are getting on, e.g., once a week. Write down your arrangement.

6 How will you reward yourself when you have completed your activity?

Figure 9.1 *A sample action plan*

Action plan

What are you going to do as a result of the training session?

1   What do you want to do? Choose a particular task or activity.

2   When will you do it?

3   Where will you do it?

4   Will you be working by yourself or with someone else? If you are working with someone else then have you obtained his or her support.

5   What will you see, hear and feel when you have achieved your goal?

6   Is there anything that will stop you from doing it? How can you prevent this from happening?

7   How will you reward yourself when you have completed your task/activity?

Figure 9.2   *A sample action plan*

AUDIOVISUAL AIDS

In the words of Kalish (1997), "Audio visual aids are used to illustrate, clarify and simplify presentations. They can enhance your presentation or ruin it."

Table 9.1 shows the advantages and disadvantages of the technique in general, and Table 9.2 those of different specific aids.

Table 9.1   *Using AV aids* (Adapted from K. Kalish, *How to give a terrific presentation,* American Management Association, 1997)

AV aids can enhance a presentation by:	AV aids can ruin it if they're:
• simplifying complex materials	• overused
• adding variety	• confusing
• clarifying certain points	• too wordy, crowded, or include too many numbers or graphs
• adding color and additional visual stimulation	• colorless, boring
• reducing the time to present	• incorrect – wrong data, spelling errors
• increasing retention	• not designed for audience/context
	• read word-for-word

Table 9.2   *Using different AV aids* (Adapted from J. Gough, *Developing learning materials,* IPD, 1996)

AV aids	Advantages	Disadvantages
Audiotapes	Easy to use Can be listened to inside training events or outside (e.g., as a post-course activity) Easy to distribute Flexible – easy to stop and start Relatively cheap Low cost equipment	Learners can be reluctant to listen Not very interactive Sophisticated recordings need to be produced professionally, which can be expensive
Computer-based presentations, e.g., PowerPoint	Look very professional Simple to edit, change sequence, etc. Can use animation Can use color, symbols, pictures	Need correct equipment Equipment/systems may fail Need a back-up Equipment/systems may not be compatible with your system Some participants may consider them "too flashy" Need lights off to view them
Computer-based training	Learner-paced Flexible and easy to use Cost-effective Convenient Consistent approach to training for each learner Relatively cheap Wide choice of packages Can be used in many different locations	Lacks personal touch Need PCs to run it on Equipment can break down Lacks personal contact There is not always a record of the learner's work

Table 9.2 *Continued*

AV aids	Advantages	Disadvantages
The Internet	Provision of online self-paced learning across the World Wide Web Online support normally available Contact with other learners Sharing of common information Information is up-to-date Easy to update Relatively inexpensive	Need to be able to access it Need to spend time researching and evaluating materials
Interactive video CD-ROM	Learner-paced Learner is fully involved Cost-effective (especially if large numbers need to be trained) Flexible and easy to use Training can be individualized Motivating and fast-moving Learner receives rapid feedback Monitors and records learner's progress Training packages can be used many times Wide choice of off-the-shelf packages Some packages can be customized CDs are portable and easy to install and store	Few programs available relevant to library world or using library examples Development and production can be lengthy and costs high Problems with compatibility and formatting sometimes exist, although these are becoming less common
Flipcharts	Can be prepared in advance Can be used to record information elicited from audience, e.g., in a brainstorming exercise Secret notes can be written (in pencil for trainer's eyes only) Can use color, symbols, pictures Place can be marked using Post-it notes Can be torn off pad and displayed on wall Useful to record findings from group exercises with groups presenting their own flipchart Can be seen in normal room light	Effective only with groups of up to about 20 Break eye contact with group when you write on them Some trainers may be concerned about their handwriting/spelling in the training context
Microphones	Allow you to be heard without raising voice	Feedback and distortion may be irritating to audience Can break down Easy to forget you have got it on so you must switch it off as soon as you stop presenting
Overhead transparencies	Can be produced using a computer application or handwritten Can use color, symbols, pictures	OHP may break down Difficult to get aligned

Table 9.2 *Continued*

AV aids	Advantages	Disadvantages
	Can be seen in normal room light	Can look amateurish
	Very portable	OHP makes a noise
Text-based materials	Cost-effective	Need to look professional
	Flexible and portable	Not as interactive as computer-based materials
	Relatively cheap to produce and update	
	Easy to use	
	Provides a record of learners' responses	
Video	Convenient, flexible and low cost	Expensive to update
	Portable	Off-the-shelf videos may not be
	Useful for portraying real-life	entirely relevant
	situations	Must be professionally produced
	Stimulates participants to ask	Realism may be lacking
	questions and to test out new	Passive medium
	approaches in the workplace	Can appear old fashioned: the content
	Provides a high-impact high-interest	is good but the actors' clothes date
	learning experience	(bell bottoms, mini skirts)
	Relatively long shelf life	Need access to video playing equipment
	Learners can stop and review	Equipment may break down
	Wide choice available	
Videoconferencing	Access to multisited locations worldwide	Expensive equipment
		Technology not very accessible
	Face-to-face support and contact with fellow learners and trainers	May not work at vital time
Whiteboard	Can be used to record information elicited from audience, e.g., in a brainstorming exercise	Only effective with a small group
		Need the correct whiteboard pens
	Can use color, symbols, pictures	
	Can wipe off and reuse	

BRAINSTORMING

Brainstorming is often used in training sessions as a means of generating ideas and discussion. The key point about brainstorming is that no responses should be questioned or challenged: every offering is recorded and written down. The technique of brainstorming involves the following steps:

1 Decide to brainstorm
2 Agree to a time limit (likely to be under five minutes)
3 Appoint a scribe to, for example, write ideas on the flipchart
4 Start brainstorming. Participants say out loud their ideas on a topic following these rules:
   • no criticism
   • allow brains to freewheel

- generate as many ideas as possible
- record every idea, however fantastic and even if it is repeated

5   At the end of the brainstorming time, take each idea and consider it in turn.

Brainstorming is often used by trainers:

- as a warm-up exercise
- to help participants focus on an issue
- to generate ideas
- to help people think creatively.

The only tools you need are paper (flipchart size if you are doing a whole group brainstorm) and pens.

EXAMPLE

The following excerpt is taken from a learning log:

" . . . we were asked to climb out of our 'boxes' and think creatively. In our group we brainstormed 156 ideas for improving security. Ideas could be silly, humorous and extremely innovative. We did not have the usual financial or I-have-got-my-manager's-hat-on constraints. We were also not allowed to squash anybody else's ideas, however much they made us laugh . . . the results were impressive and very surprising."

BUZZ GROUPS

Buzz groups are created whenever the trainer asks the participants, in pairs or very small groups, to discuss an issue or question. Feedback may or may not be provided to the whole group. Buzz groups can be used to break up lectures or presentations, and in this context they help relieve the concentration of listening. Buzz groups can also be used to help people focus on a particular issue or topic. In this case, feedback may be required.

CASE STUDIES

A case study is an example situation based on a real-life situation and it is given to participants who may be asked to:

- identify key issues
- suggest the best solution(s)
- identify how they reached their decision(s)
- identify what needs to happen next.

Table 9.3 shows the advantages and disadvantages of the technique.

Table 9.3 *Advantages and disadvantages of case studies*

Advantages	Disadvantages
May be used as an exercise during the training event or as "homework" (to be done before or during the event).	The case study may be an oversimplification of a real-life situation and this may mislead some students when they return to their own work situations.
Provide the opportunity to apply theory to practice.	Case studies often have a number of possible solutions. In training events many participants are seeking "the right answer."
Encourage communication between participants.	
Encourage peer learning.	This situation may cause tension and the trainer needs to debrief it carefully.

The case study requires:

- detailed preparation (any errors in the materials will be quickly picked up by the participants and may destroy the impact of the case study on the training event)
- possible "pilot" runs
- the trainer must be familiar with the material
- the trainer must clearly brief the participants
- the trainer must debrief and summarize the findings.

Case studies may be of varying lengths and sometimes short ones can be used very effectively. Commercially available training materials often include case studies. Case studies are likely to contain the following information:

- a description of the real-world context
- necessary forms, facts and figures
- availability of support materials
- questions to consider.

The case study materials may be provided at the start of the exercise or they may be phased, i.e., participants receive different materials and information as the situation develops.

EXAMPLE

Kendall (1990) describes the following use of example case studies as part of a "Library customer services in a multiracial society" course for library assistants in Sheffield.

Library customer services in a multiracial society: course program

9:15 am	Introduction
9:30 am	What is good customer service?

10:15 am	Break
10:30 am	Working in a multiracial society
	Video
	Discussion
12 noon	City policy and the legal framework
12:30 pm	Lunch
1:30–4:00	Looking at practical problems
	Case studies
4 pm	Action plans
4:30 pm	Course review

Looking at practical problems: example case studies

1 A Chinese man comes into the library and says something to you which you do not understand. Eventually you deduce he wants to register as a library user and you give him a form. You explain to him how to fill it in but it is obvious he does not comprehend what you are saying.

What might you do? Discuss this.

2 You are at the counter when a reader asks to reserve a new Danielle Steel book. You warn her that it might take several months to arrive and she is obviously annoyed by this. She begins to complain bitterly about the amount of Afro-Caribbean poetry on a nearby display and says that it is a waste of money and no one reads it. She pays her town taxes and she is entitled to a better service.

How would you react to this? What might you say to her? Discuss and make notes.

3 One morning an Asian reader asks to reserve a particular book on the history of Islam. It is a book which goes with a series he has been listening to on NPR. You check the shelves, the catalog and *Books in Print* and you cannot trace it. The reader complains that he can never find any recent serious books on Islam in the library.

What would you say? Discuss and make notes.

4 You are working in the children's library one afternoon when a parent with a toddler asks you why you don't have any *Little Black Sambo* books any more. She used to read them when she was little and enjoyed them. They never did her any harm. She asks if they have been banned by the library.

What would you reply? Discuss and make notes.

DEMONSTRATIONS

A useful approach to getting your point over is to actually demonstrate it. In library training sessions demonstrations may be used as part of skills development programs, for example assertiveness skills, management skills, health and safety training. Trainers need to:

- perform the demonstration themselves
- plan the demonstration carefully
- keep it simple
- provide supporting materials (handout, visual aids)
- carry out the demonstration and instruct at the same time
- provide the participants with the opportunity to practice afterward.

Table 9.4 shows the advantages and disadvantages of demonstrations.

Table 9.4 *Advantages and disadvantages of demonstrations*

Advantages	Disadvantages
Appeal to visual and auditory learners	Are of limited value to people who don't learn by observing others
Attract and hold people's attention	
Are easily understood	Pace may be too slow/quick for some learners
Are convincing	Can go wrong
	Participants may feel overwhelmed by the skill of the trainer and think that they will never achieve that level of competence

During the demonstration you need to:

- Thank any volunteers who are assisting you
- Explain to the volunteer that you will be talking to the whole group at certain times
- Describe your objectives and procedures clearly
- Describe each step
- Summarize key points. If you are being supported by a training assistant then they can write up these points on a flipchart as you work through the demonstration.

After the demonstration you should:
- Thank the volunteer (and training assistant)
- Raise questions to clarify points
- Link the demonstration to work situations
- Link the practice to theory
- Give everyone the opportunity to practice the skill or technique.

If you are using equipment then have a contingency plan for it not working.

If you are carrying out a demonstration with the help of a volunteer from the audience then be careful whom you choose. Often people who are very quick to volunteer are not the best subjects. *You* choose the person who you will feel most comfortable working with and who you think will provide the simplest and clearest demonstration material.

EXAMPLE

At a library training event on project management skills the software MS Project was going to be demonstrated. All the equipment had been tested at the start of the day when the trainer ran through the demonstration twice and it worked perfectly. Two hours later with 15 participants in front of him the demonstration didn't work. He had to use his contingency plan of pre-prepared OHP transparencies with accompanying handouts.

DISCUSSIONS

The discussion method is an excellent means of enabling everyone to participate, discuss issues, relate theory to practice and to raise objections or new issues. Discussions can be set up as:

- whole group discussions
- small group discussions
- snowball discussions (where members of one group join up with another group, they then join up with another group, and so on until everyone is working as a large group).

A key guiding principle is to start people off working in small groups early on in the event and then gradually build the training process until it is whole group working. This helps people to feel comfortable and participate fully in the training event.

EXAMPLE

An assertiveness training event was held for library assistants working in a public library. As one of the exercises on this course they were asked to work in groups of three for 15 minutes and discuss the advantages and disadvantages of being assertive, aggressive or passive while doing desk duty. They were asked to note their key points on the following handout.

Example: Assertiveness training event – discussion document

Behaviour	Advantages	Disadvantages
Assertive		
Passive		
Aggressive		

At the end of the 15 minutes, the trainer asked every group to share their key findings (these were written on a flipchart) and a group discussion followed. The small group activity gave all the participants time to think about different ideas and issues and led to a richer full group discussion.

GAMES

The distinguishing features of games are that they have a scoring mechanism to determine the winner(s) and they are played according to a fixed set of rules, i.e., rules may not be changed during the game! In a game the course participants take on the role of player and work toward winning the game by following a set of rules.

Games may be used for a variety of reasons in training sessions:

- as an energizer
- to help integrate new ideas
- to demonstrate to the learners how much they have learned
- to promote particular types of learning, e.g., teamwork
- to facilitate problem solving or creativity
- for fun.

Managing games in training sessions

> Games, exercises and simulations are not only different from each other, they are incompatible. If some people treat an event as a game while others behave as if it were an exercise or simulation then the results will be disappointing, or unpleasant, or even disastrous. It is important to know what methodology you are supposed to be in.
>
> K. Jones, *Icebreakers: a source book of games,*
> *exercises and simulations*, Kogan Page, 1991

As with all activities included in training courses, games require preparation. The time given to a particular game is likely to be relatively short, typically less than an hour. This means that the game must be relatively easy to understand and easy to set up. Sugar (1998) provides the structure for games shown in Table 9.5.

Table 9.5 *Structure of games in training events* (Adapted from S. Sugar, *Games that teach,* Jossey-Bass/Pfeiffer, 1998)

Stage	Time	Activity
Set up	25%	This time is used to introduce the game, set up the room, hand out materials, describe the rules of the game.
Play	50%	This is the time given to playing the game. This includes start and stop of play, clarifying rules, closure, e.g., declaring winners, giving out prizes.
Debrief	25%	This is the time given to process game content and player conduct. In many situations, e.g., team-building training events, this is the reason for the game, i.e., it provides real-life evidence and insights that can be translated into applications in the workplace.

Choice of games

There are a number of key questions to ask when considering a game for use:

- How does it meet the learning outcome of the session?
- Is it appropriate for this stage in the session/course?
- Do you, the trainer, fully understand the game and feel comfortable running it?

The answer to all of these questions needs to be "yes" before you proceed with using a game. My own experience is that games work providing that the trainer believes that they will work and presents them in a positive and constructive manner.

Types of games

There are many books available which describe an assortment of games that trainers may use in their training sessions. The scope for games is massive and includes:

- quizzes
- board games
- activity games, often used on team-building events, such as:
  - build the largest tower possible using a pack of cards
  - move an egg across a barrier (e.g., a table) using an assortment of equipment – glue, string, paper, etc.

EXAMPLE

Evans (1996) reviews *The Library Game* as follows:

"It had to come! A board game about library use and skills. Up to six players go round the board using the die and collecting tokens as they go. They could land on a lucky space ('You helped the librarian tidy the shelves – go forward one space') or on How much do you know? ('Can you find a book about flags in the library?') Then there is the detour into 'Mr Dewey's House.'"

The game is intended for pupils in the early years of secondary school or those in higher years who have special educational needs. It is best played in a library under supervision of a librarian, probably after a period of introduction to the library and/or a course of library and information skills, when the children have become familiar with the organization and context of their own library.

The game takes 40–60 minutes, and there are blank "How much do you know?" cards for your own questions or area of the library you wish to highlight. This game is good. It's a fun way of introducing library use and skills.

Quizzes

Quizzes are described in detail below as they are simple to set up and run in a variety of library training events. Everyone is familiar with the idea of a quiz. Using a quiz provides an easy and fun way of reviewing the content of a course, integrating learning and identifying gaps in learning. Quizzes can be set up in a number of ways:

OVERALL FORMAT

- TV game shows provide a wide range of familiar formats
- Use one of these or create your own

QUESTIONS

- Trainer can prepare a list of questions
- Participants can prepare a list of questions
- Remember to start off with easy questions
- Stack the questions for success (this is a game not an exam!)
- Questions can be serious and may also include some joke questions

QUESTION MASTER

- This may be the trainer(s)
- Alternatively the participants may ask the trainer(s) the questions!

TEAMS

- You may want to work with pairs or small groups
- Think about how you will set up the teams

ADDING FUN

- It is up to the trainer to create the learning environment
- Party hats, beepers, bells and whistles are all very effective!
- Including joke questions, tasks, etc., can also enliven the atmosphere

SCORING

- May be serious
- May be semiserious.

An increasing number of quizzes are becoming available online on the Internet.

EXAMPLE

As part of an orientation program for six new library staff there was a quiz. The new staff were asked to work in pairs and find out the answers to 30 questions by walking around the library and identifying the key features.

Example questions
- Where are the restrooms on the first floor?
- What is kept on the fourth floor?
- Whose office is near the back stairs on the second floor?
- Where are the newspapers kept?
- Whose office door is covered with pictures of Scotland?
- Where is the fire exit on the first floor?
- Where is the entrance for people in wheelchairs?
- Where are the book carts kept on the first floor?
- How many computer terminals are there in public areas?
- Where is the video library?
- Where are the patents?
- Where is the break room/cafeteria? When you have found it go and have a cup of tea or coffee. The trainer will meet you there.

EXAMPLE

As part of an in-house IT training program staff were given a quiz at the end of the course. They were asked to work in pairs and complete the quiz of 30 questions within the next ten days. They were asked to e-mail their results to the trainer. They were allowed to e-mail the trainer with questions during this time. This quiz helped to integrate their learning about IT and it also helped to transfer their new knowledge and skills into the workplace. The trainer generated a lot of enthusiasm about the quiz and, as a result, staff who were not taking the training course asked if they could join in too.

LEARNING CONTRACTS

A learning contract is an agreement between two people (or more) specifying a learning process. Learning contracts are likely to contain the following information:

- learning outcome
- proposed activity
- resources required
- support required
- assessment of learning outcomes
- target date.

Learning contracts are a useful way of formalizing a learning process and they can be tailor-made to suit individual learning requirements. They can be agreed before a learning process starts, for example at the training needs analysis stage or at the start of a particular training event.

Agreeing to a learning contract can be a motivating process as it enables the participant to explicitly commit to the learning process and it defines the outcomes of that process. Learning contracts do not have to be long or complicated documents as the example in Figure 9.3 shows.

Learning contract

Name of staff: *William Ho*

Name of trainer: *John Jones*

Date: *3/15/00*

Learning objective: *To become competent in the use of Excel.*

Proposed activities: *Revise familiarity with desktop*
Attend an Excel training course
Complete Excel open learning package
Complete online assessment
Attend 1:2:1 session with JJ.

Resources required: *Time (5 full days). Access to course. Open learning package.*

Support required: *Support from JJ. Availability of IT help desk.*

Additional needs: *Can't attend course 2nd week in April. Wife in hospital and will have childcare responsibilities.*

Assessment of learning outcomes: *Online assessment and debriefing with JJ.*

Target date: *4/30/00*

Figure 9.3 *Sample learning contract*

LECTURES

Lectures are a common means of transmitting information and providing the "big picture" on a particular topic. They are also used to provide a theoretical outline. Their advantages and disadvantages are shown in Table 9.6.

Lectures are widely used in education organizations and in these organizations library staff are likely to be involved in giving them at different times, e.g., student orientation, introduction to skills training units. The information presented in the section on presentations (pp. 173–4) is all very relevant to lectures.

Table 9.6 *Advantages and disadvantages of lectures*

Advantages	Disadvantages
Students find them reassuring	Students are passive
Efficient use of time	Cannot accommodate individual learning needs
Can provide overview of subject/theoretical framework	Student recall of subject tends to be poor
Can inspire students	Can turn students off

MIND MAPPING

Mind mapping is a useful tool for learning. It is a simple technique which can be learned in less than five minutes and is fun to do. The idea was developed by Tony Buzan (1989) as an aid to accelerating learning and enhancing creativity. Mind maps work because they involve both sides of the brain: the left-hand side through the logical arrangement of ideas and the right-hand side through the use of color, symbols and pictures.

In training sessions mind maps may be used as an individual or group activity. They are a very practical and active way to help someone to learn. People who find it hard to get started on a piece of work often find that mind maps help to get their ideas flowing. The purpose of using mind maps on training events is to help:

- organize ideas
- generate ideas
- develop a memory aid
- integrate learning.

As a group activity they are very useful as a means of enabling a group to identify and organize lots of different ideas. They encourage small group interaction as everyone in a small group can be working on the mind map together.

How to mind map

All you need to mind map is lots of different colored felt tip pens and also some large pieces of paper, for example flipchart paper or the back of wallpaper. The key features of a mind map include:

1 You start with the central idea and write it in the middle of the page. Add a picture or a symbol. Use two or three colors.
2 You draw some large bold branches leading off from the central idea. Along each one write the key ideas in large letters. Use different colors for each idea but keep the size of the branches and the letters the same.
3 Draw smaller branches leading from each key word. These are for connected but less important ideas. Use color, pictures and symbols to make your mind map look interesting.
4 You then can add even smaller branches and these may be colored and illustrated with little pictures or symbols.

EXAMPLE

The final activity on an assertiveness training course involved the participants working in groups of four developing their own mind map on the theme of "Assertiveness at work." The trainer explained the basic rules of mind mapping and gave each group ten felt tip pens and also a piece of flipchart paper. The groups had 15 minutes to develop their mind map. The resulting mind maps were displayed on the wall and everyone admired them. Looking at the mind maps gave the trainer useful information on which topics the participants considered important and those that they had missed out. She used this information as part of the course evaluation process.

PACKAGED LEARNING PROGRAMS

Packaged learning programs enable learners to have control over:

- what they learn
- when they learn it
- where they learn it
- their pace of learning.

Packaged learning programs may include printed, audiovisual, computer-based learning materials. They may be stand-alone packages or they may be provided with support, e.g., by phone, e-mail, help desk, tutorial. There are many commercial packages and these cover a wide range of topics and themes. In addition, many information and library services develop their own in-house packages to suit the particular needs of their staff.

Packaged learning programs can be used at different stages in the training process:

- as a precourse preparatory activity
- as an on-course activity (working independently, in small groups or with the trainer)
- as a postcourse activity.

It is important that the trainer explains the rationale for the use of the packaged program in the context of the particular training process, otherwise there is the potential danger that the participants feel cheated and that the trainer isn't doing their job.

EXAMPLE

As part of a five-day orientation program new library staff spent time working through a series of short learning packages on topics such as using the circulation system and basic information searching skills. They were allocated two hours for using each package and worked in pairs. At the end of this time they were debriefed by their team leader. They were able to keep the learning packages as a reference tool.

EXAMPLE

Library staff in a university delivered all the basic IT skills programs to students. These were delivered by a series of workshops and each workshop was supported by a packaged learning program. The trainer introduced the session, handled any questions or problems, managed the online assessment process, and ended the session. The use of the learning packages (which were printed and available online) meant that students could work at their own pace. Fifteen library staff were involved in this activity and the delivery method meant that they provided a high quality and consistent series of workshops. It also meant that staff development for new library trainers was relatively simple.

PRACTICAL EXERCISES

Practical exercises give the participants the opportunity to practice their skills and they may be carried out individually or in groups. Practical exercises may be used to:

- integrate learning
- practice skills
- relate theory to practice.

Figure 9.4 gives an example taken from a one-day course on project management. The exercise was used as part of a session on finance. The

Project management course – Costing labor exercise

BASIC FORMULA

Daily rate = (Annual salary+benefits)/(working days per year)

Working days per year = Days in year − (annual leave + weekends + legal holidays + sick days)
= 365 − (20 + 104 + 11 + 10) = 216 per year, i.e., 18 days per month.

WORKED EXAMPLE

What is the cost of a Systems Officer working on a special project for 2 days per month for 12 months?

Annual salary	=	$40,000
Benefits	=	$8,000
Number of working days per year	=	216
Number of days on project	=	24

Daily rate = ($40,000 + $8,000)/(216)	=	$222.22

Cost for 24 days = $222.22 × 24	=	$5333.33

EXERCISE EXAMPLE

What is the cost of a Publications Manager working on a special project for 5 days per month for 12 months?

Annual salary	=	$35,000
Benefits	=	$7,000
Number of working days per annum	=	216
Number of days on project	=	60

Daily rate	=	

Cost for _____ days	=	

Figure 9.4 *Sample practical exercise (Adapted from K. Black, Project management for library and information professionals, Aslib, 1996)*

trainer explained the key ideas about costing labor and then worked through example 1 on the flipchart. She then asked the participants to work in pairs and work through the second example. Answers were shared in the whole group with the trainer and this was followed by a general discussion.

The exercise in Figure 9.5 was used on a training skills course aimed at library and IT support staff who provide skills training courses for university students. The session was on using lectures and after a 20-minute presentation followed by a question and answer session, the group was asked to work in pairs or trios. They were then given the handout in the figure. Their task was to identify one or more responses to the situations. After 15 minutes the group as a whole worked through the answers and discussed issues that arose from the exercise.

LECTURES/PRESENTATIONS   **HANDOUT**

How would you deal with the following situations?

1   You sense that the students are becoming restless and inattentive. One or two whispered conversations have begun and some have clearly stopped making notes.
2   Whenever you ask your audience a question, you are met with a wall of silence.
3   A group of students talk to you after a presentation and tell you that it is difficult to make notes in your lecture.
4   You have a large number of handouts to distribute before and during your lecture.
5   You want to get feedback from the students on your performance as a lecturer.
6   At the beginning of your lecture and whenever you have given students time to discuss issues, you find it difficult to gain their attention.
7   The OHP breaks down.
8   The video doesn't work.
9   A student becomes ill.
10   You "dry up."
11   Some students say that they have already covered the topic. Others have not covered it before.
12   Students say that they are only there because it is compulsory.

Figure 9.5   *Sample practical exercise*

PRESENTATIONS

Presentations are an ideal method for introducing the course participants to key ideas and themes. Hackett (1997) says, "The effectiveness of a presentation depends on the clarity of its objectives and the extent to which the audience buy into them." She describes the characteristics of effective presenters as:

- clear and pleasant speaking voice
- no distracting verbal mannerisms
- personal "presence"
- empathy with and interest in your audience
- effective questioning skills.

Presentation skills are covered in detail in Chapter 3.

Table 9.7 shows the advantages and disadvantages of presentations.

Table 9.7 *Advantages and disadvantages of presentations*

Advantages	Disadvantages
Participants expect them	Require extensive preparation
Can provide a useful starting point to an event	Some participants may already be familiar with the subject
Useful way of providing an overview or framework	matter
Can bring the group together	Some participants may not feel involved in presentation
Can be delivered with a minimum of aids (although properly used these enhance the presentation)	Limited to relatively short time periods (up to 20 minutes)
Can build in interactive elements and question and answer sessions	
Trainer can adapt presentation to meet needs of particular audience	
Trainer can pace and lead group into a learning state	

The Library Association in the UK (1999) has published a resource, *Presentation skills for library and information professionals*, which provides a modular two-day program including 15 separate sessions on topics such as:

- importance of effective communication
- barriers to effective communication
- presentation practices
- what makes a good presentation
- dealing with stress and anxiety
- audience analysis
- aims and objectives
- planning the structure
- visual aids
- delivery
- action planning.

This package may be used by library trainers for running internal courses on presentation skills.

QUESTION AND ANSWER SESSIONS

Question and answer sessions are a useful way of generating energy, integrating learning, assessing learning and having fun. Questioning techniques are covered in Chapter 3. The sessions can be used in a variety of ways:

- Trainer leads a group question and answer session.
- Participants work in pairs and each pair prepares at least one question. These are written on a card and given to the trainer. The whole group then works toward answering all the questions with the support of the trainer.
- Trainer has pre-prepared questions on a worksheet. Participants work in twos and threes and answer the questions. There is a whole group debriefing session.
- Individuals or pairs work through a series of online questions.

QUESTIONING

Questioning is an important trainer's skill and is explored in Chapter 4 (pp. 87–91). The use of questions to promote reflection is explored on p. 96.

The trainer needs to decide when he/she wants to receive questions during their training event – at any time, or when they ask for them? Let the participants know at the start of the event which is your preferred method of handling questions.

At the same time, it is worthwhile having a questioning strategy prepared for your training event. Pre-prepared questions are often useful and help limit "thinking on your feet."

EXAMPLE

Remember your audience. The author recently observed a library staff training event with a group of 20 staff, i.e., the whole staff from a special library. Throughout the day the trainer asked the whole group some excellent questions. On the whole, these were responded to by the team leaders, deputy librarian and librarian. Other staff, e.g., library assistants, shelvers and technicians, did not answer the questions. One of the feedback points in the course evaluations was that the library assistants felt intimidated about answering questions in the whole group as they were not used to being in a large group or meeting. The trainer needed to change his approach to the use of questions during this type of event to ensure that everyone was able to respond to questions, e.g., by asking people to discuss the answer with their neighbors and then give a joint response.

QUESTIONNAIRES

Questionnaires may be used as a self-assessment or a group assessment and they will provide a framework for discussion. Questionnaires may be completed before a training event, during the event or after the training event.

Key points about using questionnaires include:

- How do they help you to meet the learning outcomes of the event?
- Is their length appropriate, i.e., not too long?
- Is their language appropriate?
- Will you provide pencils or pens?
- How will they be debriefed?
- How will the learning be processed?
- What will you do if some people complete it very quickly, e.g., in five minutes, while others take 20 minutes? How will you manage that time difference?

EXAMPLE

The example learning style questionnaire presented on pp. 28–30 was used in a half-day workshop on work-based learning for college staff. The trainer introduced the idea of learning styles and then handed out the questionnaire (with pencils) and asked everyone to fill it in. As participants finished the questionnaire the trainer suggested that they find someone else who had finished and compare and contrast their results.

Once everyone had finished the questionnaire then they were asked to form groups based on their results, e.g., all activists together, all reflectors together, etc. They were then asked to discuss their findings and their likes/dislikes about learning. These were written up on a flipchart and each group presented their findings to the whole group. One interesting point that emerged was that the activists all completed the questionnaire first!

The trainer then debriefed the whole process and answered any questions. Finally, she gave a "health warning" and pointed out the dangers of labelling people through this type of activity. She highlighted how flexible everyone is and how our learning styles develop and change over time.

ROLE PLAYS

Role plays may be used to integrate theory and practice. They are widely used in skills training courses, e.g., in interviewing, appraisal training, mentoring training. In a role play, participants are assigned a particular role and asked to work through a problem, situation or process while staying in this role. Role plays are potentially very powerful and if they involve participants handling emotional or potentially emotive situations then it is important that the trainer is experienced in facilitating and debriefing this type of process. Table 9.8 shows their advantages and disadvantages.

Table 9.8   *Advantages and disadvantages of role play*

Advantages	Disadvantages
Involves active participation of participants	Some participants hate it and will not engage in it
Provides an opportunity to practice a skill in a "safe" environment	Participants may overact and exaggerate their roles so that the role play degenerates into a farce
Provides a real link between theory and practice	There is a risk involved. Once the role play has started it is the participants who lead the activity.
Enhances interpersonal skills	May generate high levels of emotion that need to be channelled and processed
May generate ideas and issues that participants were not previously aware of	Requires sensitive debriefing
Provides a forum for increasing self-awareness and reflection	Participants may dismiss it as "acting" and not see the connection with real life

EXAMPLE

In a performance management training event library team leaders were asked to role play a manager and a challenging member of staff. They were given the following scenario:

SCENARIO

This is the first performance management meeting between Chris and Sandy.

Chris has managed the team in an industrial information unit for five years. S/he is always eager to take on new ideas and hopes that the new performance management system will improve staff motivation and performance. S/he has attended three separate one-day training events on the new system. Her/his main objective for her/his meeting with Sandy is to get him/her to commit to the process and to complete form PM1 in a meaningful manner.

Sandy is an excellent information worker. S/he believes her/his main job is serving the research staff in the company and has little time for other activities. S/he likes to work independently and is very cynical about "the latest management fads." S/he thinks everyone would achieve more work if they spent all their time working rather than talking about it. Sandy attended the compulsory performance management training events where s/he let her/his views be known. Sandy's main aim for the first meeting is to let Chris know how stupid s/he thinks the new system is. Sandy is unwilling to commit to any specific objectives on the grounds that they will mean s/he will be limited in the type of work s/he can do.

The first meeting is based around the following form (p. 177).

INSTRUCTIONS

Work in groups of three participants. One person takes on the role of Chris and another person takes on the role of Sandy. The third person is an observer. Each group will role play the situation three times as this will give everyone the opportunity to rotate roles. Spend 15 minutes on each role play followed by a five-minute discussion. The whole role play will take an hour.

NEW WORLD COMPANY

PERFORMANCE MANAGEMENT PROCESS FORM: PM1

Name of employer: _____ **Name of manager:** _____

Key questions

1 Complete a SWOT analysis on the basis of your last year's work in the company.

SWOT analysis	
Strengths	Weaknesses
Opportunities	Threats

2 Identify your main aim for the forthcoming year.

3 Identify 5 specific work objectives.

4 Identify other issues that need to be discussed/tackled.

SIMULATIONS

A simulation is an activity where a real-life situation is simulated and the participants are provided with details of the library, events and individuals. It is a highly structured activity and the participants are expected to work through the simulation so that they learn from this experience. At the end, a debriefing session explores the learning that has taken place.

EXAMPLE

A library course on disaster planning included a simulation exercise that lasted three hours. It was a simulation of a major flood in a public library. The library managers had to make key decisions and direct operations on the basis of the information presented to them. As the exercise progressed the trainers provided them with changing circumstances plus additional information. The debriefing at the end of the simulation included reflection on their decision making, communications strategy, teamwork and coordination of people and resources.

SMALL GROUPS

This is the name given to an activity where participants work in small groups on a particular task and then report back to the main groups. Each small group can work on the same or a different task.

The task needs to be carefully structured and each group needs to be given clear instructions on the purpose of their task, what they are expected to achieve, the process that they need to go through, and the way in which they need to report back. Time-keeping needs to be mentioned here too. The trainer's role during the small group activity is to make sure that the different groups are on course and to ensure that everyone gets back on time.

If the groups are meeting in different rooms throughout a building then some time is lost as everyone moves to their room and settles down before they start their work. At the end of their task they then have to rejoin the group and settle down again. If there are people in the group with limited mobility this can cause them personal difficulties, so it needs to be handled appropriately.

SNOWBALLING

This technique is often used in conferences or training events that involve very large groups of library staff. Snowballing is a technique that enables large groups of delegates to share ideas or work through a particular process. It enables delegates to work with a large number of people in a structured and relatively safe manner. The basic technique involves people working in small groups that join up with other groups so that by the end of the process everyone is working together in one large group. Everyone stays in the same original group and this helps to provide safety and security for individual participants. The participants are given a series of tasks and asked to work in the following sequence:

- individually
- in pairs (sharing individual responses)
- in fours (share again, compare and contrast their responses)
- in the full group with each group of four contributing.

This technique can be used with a wide range of possible tasks and topics. It is a useful icebreaking technique for the start of an event. It is a very flexible technique as stages, such as pairs, can be missed out or added, e.g., groups of four combine to eight people. However, each stage needs to be different from the previous stage, otherwise it becomes repetitive and boring.

STORIES AND METAPHORS

The power of storytelling has been known for centuries. Stories, metaphors and anecdotes are frequently used in training events as a means of:

- providing inspiration
- illustrating a point
- stimulating creativity
- stimulating problem solving
- introducing complex ideas
- bypassing the conscious mind
- energizing the participants
- providing an element of relaxation.

Stories, metaphors or anecdotes may be used at any stage in the learning process and they only need to last a few minutes. Indeed weaving together a number of small metaphors or stories is often more effective than telling one story which lasts 35 minutes! Stories and metaphors stimulate both sides of the brain: the left-hand side takes in the words and the order of ideas, while the right-hand side responds to imagination, visualization and creativity.

Strategies for constructing and presenting metaphors can be obtained by studying oral traditions such as storytelling. The work of traditional storytellers is a balance between remembrance and improvization, i.e., knowing how to tell a story in a way that it can be retained. This involves using rhythm, repetition, surprising twists, mnemonics, creating stimulating images, sounds or feelings, and linking the story to what is familiar and important to the listener.

Overdurf and Silverthorn (1995) provide the following strategy for using stories and metaphors:

1 Find a story, incident, or slice of life which has had an impact on you.
2 Read it over or go over it once mentally.
3 Let it settle in – at least overnight.
4 Recall it again and notice.
     – What are the major themes?
     – What other associations (other incidents, stories, etc.) do they stimulate in you?
5 Let it settle in – again, overnight.
6 Tell the story. Realize it's a "once-only" performance. The next time you tell it will be different.

Planning to use stories and metaphors

Parkin (1998) provides an extremely useful guide to using stories and metaphors to facilitate learning. She provides the following checklist as a guide to thinking through the use of metaphors and stories in a training event:

• What purpose do I want this story to serve – inspire, educate, illustrate a point, energize or relax the recipient?
• Does storytelling fit in with this organization's culture?
• What type of story will be most appropriate – folktale, personal anecdote, myth?
• What message am I trying to convey – communication, teamwork, motivation?
• What particular story might help their understanding right now?
• Is there a metaphor that would help them see things a different way?
• Should I read a story or just retell it in my own words?

Parkin also provides a detailed guide to using stories in training events, together with 50 example stories.

EXAMPLE

A trainer was delivering the final session of a 20-day management development program. The atmosphere was upbeat with lots of humor and excitement. Before lunch on the final day the trainer said that she'd brought something in to show the group. It was her collection of kaleidoscopes to which she had made reference at various stages of the course. She began to get the kaleidoscopes out of the box and passed them around the group. The last two kaleidoscopes were very special ones and had a series of filters which could be inserted into their main body. This provided an almost unlimited range of "pictures" in the kaleidoscope. The trainer made the point that by using these kaleidoscopes it was possible to create anything that was needed. She also said that she had stopped collecting them as she had achieved the perfect collection with lots of flexibility and options. In this way the trainer let the managers know that they now had all the skills needed to work as effective managers. It is possible that many of the managers did not pick up this message at a conscious level.

EXAMPLE

A library introduced a new appraisal system and its implementation was supported by a staff training and development program. One of the learning sessions was on action planning. As part of this session the trainer read a story from *Winnie-the-Pooh on Success* (Allen and Allen, 1998). The story was called "In which Pooh and The Stranger are stuck, everyone sets goals and Alexander Beetle begins to achieve one." The story was very well received – it provided some light relief as well as including some good learning points.

10
Running learning groups

INTRODUCTION

In this chapter we will focus on the people side of training events. In particular the following topics are covered:

- beginning group sessions
- climate-building
- working with group processes
- working with challenging people
- dealing with unexpected situations
- learning transfer
- ending group sessions.

Trainers can work in either a very directive or facilitative way and it is worthwhile knowing which emphasis is appropriate to which situation. This is summarized in Table 10.1.

Table 10.1   *The directive–facilitative continuum* (Adapted from F. and R. Bee, *Facilitation skills*, IPD, 1998)

Directive ⬅ ➡	**Facilitative**
Use when:	**Use when:**
working with immature groups that are inexperienced at working together	working with mature groups that are experienced at working in a facilitative way
aims and objectives are unclear and will be difficult to clarify	aims and objectives are clear or capable of clarification
there are very tight time constraints	sufficient time is available or can be made available to meet the aims and objectives
the culture/atmosphere is one of suspicion and insecurity	the culture/atmosphere is one of openness and trust
the policy toward information is one of limited access and concealment	the policy toward information is one of accessibility and transparency
your facilitation skills are undeveloped	you are confident in your facilitation skills

BEGINNING GROUP SESSIONS (adapted from Jensen 1998)

[Note: This section is adapted from Jensen, 1998.] Here is what to do in the time before the event starts:

1 Arrive at least half an hour before the event starts.
2 Arrange the furniture.
3 Display flowers, posters, etc.
4 Check that the equipment works.
5 Check the catering arrangements.
6 Find the emergency exits.
7 Find the restrooms and other facilities.
8 Lay out your resources: handouts, pens, etc.
9 Start music.
10 Check the room out using the three perceptual positions.
11 Energize yourself.
12 Be prepared to meet and greet everyone.

What to do in the first 60 seconds

I Look relaxed and well prepared

First impressions count. As the course participants arrive they are likely to look at you and make judgments about your ability as a trainer. It is vital that you look relaxed and well prepared for the training event. This will signal to the participants that you are in control of the event and that effort has been put into making this course a special event.

2 Welcome everyone to the event

Greet people and make eye contact with them. Use positive enthusiastic language such as "I'm really pleased to be here today. I'm looking forward to getting to know you and to work with you. We are going to have an interesting and enjoyable day."

3 Start enthusiastically and with energy

It is important to start with enthusiasm and energy. This will help to engage people's interest. The use of music, visual stimuli (e.g., flowers, a video projecting without sound) and movement all help to enthuse people and suggest that they are going to be having an interesting training event.

4 Get people involved

Use an icebreaker. This will help everyone to settle down and give them the opportunity to speak. My own experience is that it is best to get everyone to say something in the group as early as possible in the session (preferably within the first ten minutes). This facilitates discussion and questions during the following program. The trick is to create a safe atmosphere so everyone can speak without feeling embarrassed. See "20 ways to involve everyone in the training event" below.

5 GRAB PEOPLE'S INTEREST

Use appropriate humor to set the scene and help reduce tension in the room. Stories, jokes, a brief clip from a video or a quick quiz may all be used to grab attention.

5 ways to kill your session before you have really got going

1 LOOK UNPROFESSIONAL

If you are scruffily dressed then the course participants are likely to make negative judgments about you. On one course I attended the trainer had the remains of breakfast splattered down his tie. While this provided a topic of conversation at the break it resulted in his losing credibility before he had started. It is important to dress appropriately for the occasion and to match the dress code of the group.

2 FAIL TO PREPARE AND CHECK THE WORKING ORDER OF THE ROOM/FACILITIES/EQUIPMENT

Starting the session by asking participants to move tables/chairs, or having to ask for help with the equipment is not conducive to creating a learning environment. Ideally everything should be prepared and double-checked at least half an hour before the program starts.

3 START WITH NEGATIVE COMMENTS

If you are attending a course and the trainer starts off with comments such as, "I've just been asked to do this at the last minute and I haven't had time to prepare," "I hope you won't find it as boring as the last group," "I don't know about you but I'd prefer to be watching the tennis rather than participating in a course about . . .," "I always hate training in this room. It is too small/hot/cold," then you are likely to find it very off-putting. As trainers it is important that we start off with positive and enthusiastic comments. This means that when working as a trainer it is important to leave personal negative feelings outside the training room.

4 START LATE

Starting late means getting off to a bad start. If you are unable to start on time then explain to the group and say when you are going to start, e.g.,

"Thank you for being here on time. It is now time to start but only half the group have arrived. This could be because of a major traffic jam. I am going to give them an additional ten minutes to arrive and then we will start."

5 START TOO SLOWLY

If you get off to a slow start, e.g., your introduction is slow and lacks energy, or you go through an administrative process which is time-consuming and boring, then this means that the course has got off to a bad start. It can be hard to retrieve this situation and move into an energetic learning session. It is worthwhile planning your start in detail and rehearsing it. If there are any administrative activities that need to take place then do them later in the course (or even better do them before the course starts).

20+ ways to involve everyone in the training event

1   At the start of the session ask people what they want from the course. Write their replies on a flipchart. Then provide them with that plus more. At the end of the session refer back to the original flipchart and check that people have achieved their goals.
2   Set up an introductory activity or icebreaker.
3   Use people's names.
4   Refer to comments that participants have made earlier in the training course.
5   Demonstrate your active listening through your body and verbal language.
6   Treat everyone with respect.
7   Be culturally sensitive.
8   Use all the senses – visual, auditory, kinesthetic.
9   Encourage learning in different groups, e.g., pairs, trios, asking people to work with people they haven't already worked with or those who are the same height as themselves, etc.
10 Have breaks and use these to reenergize with, e.g., simple Brain Gym exercises, or a five-minute walk outside.
11 Use real-life examples.
12 Use relevant stories.
13 Use appropriate humor.
14 Use different resources – books, articles, video clips, computer-based learning.
15 Introduce fun, e.g., games and quizzes.
16 Make the learning challenging and safe.
17 Ensure that everyone feels well cared for.
18 Give people time to tell "their story" (if these aren't relevant to the training event then this sometimes needs to take place in the breaks).

19   Make sure that everyone is comfortable.

20   Use rewards – candy, boxes of chocolates, prize books.

21   Give lots of generous encouragement and praise.

5 approaches to creating a learning atmosphere

1 CREATE AN INVITING PHYSICAL ENVIRONMENT

Use flowers, music, posters, etc. Check physical comfort, e.g., room temperature. If you are aware that some of the participants have physical disabilities, for example back problems, then check that they are comfortable and give explicit permission for them to stand up, move or lie down if that will help them.

2 CREATE AN OPEN AND WELCOMING GROUP ENVIRONMENT

Arrange the chairs in a horseshoe. If you must use tables then arrange them in a relaxed "bistro" style.

3 GUIDE THE PARTICIPANTS THROUGH THE LEARNING PROCESS

Let everyone know of the plans for the day – there is no need to keep them secret. It is very important to let people know the housekeeping arrangements, e.g., times of breaks or lunch. It is sometimes worth saying that "we are all adult learners so if you need a comfort break then slip out of the room at an appropriate moment."

4 USE POSITIVE LANGUAGE

Use positive enthusiastic language – this will help people to be relaxed and confident about their learning. Thank people for their comments and questions. Use phrases such as "Great question, thank you for that welcome reminder."

5 BE ACCESSIBLE

Let them know that you are human too! Provide appropriate information about yourself, use personal anecdotes, for example about your experiences of learning/applying the material. Be available during the breaks, lunch and at the end of the course. If you need a little privacy to recharge your batteries then make it clear that this is what is happening, e.g., go for a walk.

Using icebreakers

At the start of a learning session, and particularly with a new group, there is a need to "break the ice" and to enable participants to start to meet and work together. Icebreakers can be useful tools for dispelling anxiety and tension. They are also used to raise energy levels in a group. Icebreakers are generally short activities which:

- help to get everyone involved
- help participants to get to know each other
- help to set the climate for the learning session.

It is important that the icebreaker is acceptable to the group, for example some people may be threatened by icebreakers which involve physical contact or they may be dismissive of the activity (and perhaps the trainer) if it does not appear to be relevant to the session.

SAMPLE ICEBREAKERS

1 *Meeting someone new.* Work in pairs. Choose someone you don't know. Find out who they are, why they are here, what they want from the session. Introduce your partner to the whole group. (10–20 mins.)

2 *Snowball hello.* Work in pairs. Choose someone you don't know. Find out who they are, why they are here, what they want from the session. Each pair then joins up with another pair. Introduce your partner to the foursome. Then join another pair and repeat the exercise until everyone has been introduced. (10–30 mins.)

3 *Knots.* Ask everyone to close their eyes and begin to move towards the center of the room. When they meet someone else take a hold of their hand. Once everyone is holding hands then open eyes and start to untangle the knot. (5 mins.)

4 *Name game 1.* Ask everyone to sit in a circle. Ask one person to start the process and call out a name with an associated activity, e.g., "I am Barbara and I like bananas." The next person repeats the first person's name and follows it with their own, e.g., "I am Jane and I like jelly." Once the list has got to six to eight names (depending on the confidence of the group) then start a new list. This process is repeated until everyone has had a turn. (10–15 mins.)

5 *Name game 2.* Participants sit in a circle and there is a round where everyone says their name. It may be worthwhile asking people not to go too quickly. The trainer throws a ball (or bean bag) into the circle and asks one (named) person to pass it to someone else while calling out the name of the person who receives the ball. This is repeated from person to person. It is important to keep the ball moving and to make sure that everyone is included in the activity. Continue until everyone is familiar with everybody's name. (5–10 mins.)

6 *Name game 3.* This can be used with a group of up to about 25 people. The first person introduces him or herself. The next person says "This is X [the person who has just introduced him or herself] and my

name is . . . ." The next person repeats the first and second persons' names and then introduces themselves. This process continues and is likely to end in laughter. It is a good icebreaker and can be used to introduce humor very early in the course. (10–15 mins.)

7 *Finding out about each other*. This is a simple exercise which involves everyone meeting other members of the group and obtaining answers to six questions. The questions could be at a fairly trivial level, for example do you like dogs, or they could be questions relevant to the content of the learning program. The trainer has to prepare the questions in advance and display them during the activity. (10–15 mins.)

8 *Simple icebreaker*. Ask everyone to introduce themselves by saying their name and what they want from the learning session. (5–10 mins.)

CLIMATE BUILDING

During the session, the trainer needs to create, monitor and maintain a climate that helps participants learn. Toward the end of the session, the trainer needs to signal the forthcoming ending and change the climate into one that is appropriate for learners who may be moving back into a variety of environments, for example working at a busy help desk, leading a meeting, travel, home.

A wide range of factors may affect the group climate and may help to create a positive enthusiastic climate or a dull and flat climate. Most people learn best when they feel comfortable, relaxed, interested and safe. Identifying the factors which affect the climate of a group enables teachers and trainers to influence the climate and create positive learning atmospheres. Key factors are identified below.

Factors which affect the group climate

PHYSICAL FACTORS

- room – amount of space, temperature, comfortable chairs (and tables), light, fresh air
- physical comfort – breaks, access to refreshments and restrooms
- physical access – easy access for people with additional needs, e.g., wheelchair users

TRAINER

- personality – unfriendly/neutral/friendly, tense/relaxed, optimistic/pessimistic

- training style – organized/disorganized, clear/muddled, helpful/unhelpful
- attention – to individual needs, to group needs, to tasks, to self

PARTICIPANTS

- reasons for being there – e.g., personal choice, sent by a manager, wants to gain qualification
- prelearning session experiences, e.g., has worked a 4-hour session at a busy IT help desk, a game of tennis
- postlearning session experiences, e.g., a long journey home, the start of a week's holiday
- level of interest
- level of commitment
- level of participation
- influence with other participants and/or trainer
- feelings about other participants, trainer or key people in their lives
- feelings about subject/task
- feelings about being in a learning situation
- recent life experiences, e.g., bereavement, getting a new job
- emotional states
- energy levels

GROUP

General atmosphere:

- formal/informal
- competitive/cooperative
- hostile/supportive
- inhibited/permissive
- including/excluding
- positive/negative
- structured/unstructured
- existence of subgroups or cliques
- management of task
- moving forward/blocking
- keeping focused/unfocused
- sharing/competing

TASK

- clarity of task
- participants' commitment to task

- level of risk involved in task
- trainers' familiarity with task
- content of task
- relevance of task

How to develop rapport in a group

The start of a training session is very important as it sets the climate and, to a certain extent, determines the mood for the whole session. The starting processes – welcoming, introducing and icebreaking – are all important components of setting the climate. Individual learners need to:

- feel welcomed
- feel that they are entering an enjoyable experience
- feel that they will gain what they want and need from the session
- feel that they will be given appropriate attention
- feel that they will be encouraged to develop in a positive manner.

The process of developing a conducive environment requires the ability to build rapport. This key trainer skill is described in detail in Chapter 4.

How to monitor the learning environment

It is important to monitor the learning environment so that you are aware of what is and is not happening. This means that you are then able to respond to individuals and the group, and facilitate the learning processes that are taking place. Monitoring can take place with a number of different foci:

- whole group
- individuals
- trainer.

The monitoring process involves observation skills, using sensory acuity and different perceptual positions, and these are all described in detail in Chapter 4. In addition, peripheral vision (also described in Chapter 4) is a useful tool for picking up what is happening in the training event. The type of information that may be picked up by the trainer includes:

- energy levels of the group (low, medium, high)
- energy levels of trainer (low, medium, high)
- levels of interest in the training material (low, medium, high)
- level of humor in the group (low, medium, high)
- focus of attention of individuals (self, others, trainer, training materials, elsewhere)

- participation levels in group discussions (low, medium, high)
- participation levels in exercises (low, medium, high).

This type of information is vital if the trainer is to provide a quality training event. It will influence the way you facilitate each stage of the learning process. The types of activity needed to facilitate different group processes are described below.

10 WAYS TO ENERGIZE A GROUP

1 Change your pace. Become upbeat. Use an interested and excited tone of voice. Move about more.
2 Ask the participants to do an exercise that involves moving about (even if it is only to find someone else to work with).
3 Use activities which involve competition, excitement and humor.
4 Use loud exciting music.
5 Have a break. If possible go outside for a few minutes.
6 Do some exercises, e.g., Brain Gym ones.
7 Walk and learn – ask people to get into pairs and walk outside for five minutes while they share their key learning of the day.
8 Creative handshakes – ask everyone to shake hands with three others in the group, each time inventing a new way of shaking hands.
9 Ask people to work in threes or fours and to mind map their learning for the day.
10 Ask the participants to develop a quiz of 20 questions – they need to appoint a question master and design the questions, the trainer(s) will be the quiz participant(s). Then ask them to run the quiz.

5+ APPROACHES TO CALMING DOWN A GROUP

1 Slow down your pace. Slow down your breathing.
2 Give the participants something to read, e.g., a relevant article or newspaper clipping.
3 Ask everyone to complete an activity by themselves, e.g., complete a questionnaire.
4 Give them a challenging activity to complete.
5 Tell them a story.
6 Do some calming exercises that promote concentration.

8 APPROACHES TO INCREASING PARTICIPATION IN THE GROUP PROCESS

1 Spend time building rapport with everyone.
2 Ask people to work in small groups (twos or threes).
3 As the program progresses, increase the size of the groups (see Snowballing in Chapter 9, pp. 178–9).

4   Provide activities in which everyone has a role.
5   Encourage people to participate.
6   Ask people to work in different groups.
7   Ask them what they need to help them participate in the group.
8   Check to see if you are doing something that has switched people off. If you are then do something different.

WORKING WITH GROUP PROCESSES

Research into many different kinds of groups suggests that in all groups certain kinds of process take place. An understanding of these underlying processes is helpful to trainers as it can help inform our ways of managing and working with groups. In this section we will look at the life cycle of a group.

All groups have been found to go through a life cycle (see Rodwell, 1994) and this is often described as follows:

- forming
- storming
- norming
- performing
- mourning.

Knowing where a group is in the development process is very useful as it means that when we are planning sessions we are able to include activities and approaches which are in tune with the group and help them to develop further. Sometimes a group will become "stuck" in a particular stage, for example a group which meets once a week and has a constantly changing set of members may never get beyond the forming stage. In this case, a trainer may want to develop activities which match and lead the group further.

According to Hunter (1992) most groups don't move beyond the norming stage and group members settle for "this is how it is" or "courses are always like this." They may begin to lose their enthusiasm for the course and attendance begins to drop off. Sometimes this phase coincides with the build up to exams. At other times, individual group members may start to look "for a better course" or "a more effective teacher or trainer."

Stages in the life of a group

I FORMING

The first stage. Individuals may feel anxious, uncertain or defensive. They may feel confident, enthusiastic and anxious to get started. This stage is frequently marked by individuals asking themselves the following questions: Have I made the right decision? Will I be liked? What will the others be like? In this stage, people begin to get to know each other and they may rush into one-to-one relationships or cliques. This stage is sometimes called the "honeymoon period" – and participants will make statements such as "this is the best course/trainer/group."

Useful activities: make introductions, set ground rules, allow time for a refreshment break, make doubly clear that briefings are clearly understood.

2 STORMING

At this stage conflicts between group members may become apparent as individuals want to make "their mark" on the group. The limits of behavior may be tested out. Some learners may be rebellious either by action or inaction. Participants may challenge their trainer's authority. Suggestions for activities may be challenged or rejected. There may be complaints about the course, course members or the trainer.

Useful activities: mix socially with the group to build rapport and help prevent a "them and us" situation, set up activities which involve different group members working together.

3 NORMING

At this stage, people begin to settle down and get on with the task. The unwritten rules or "norms" of the group develop. Conflict is replaced by cooperation and learners start to talk about "us" and "we." Cliques no longer exist and the group is comfortable about working in different subgroups. There is a sense of "team spirit" and humor will be present during the session.

Useful activities: allow the group more scope to make their own choices and decisions, offer and encourage feedback at a more meaningful level.

4 PERFORMING

There is a high level of trust within the group. Individuals accept each other and their strengths and weaknesses. There is a strong commitment to achieving the group goals. Few groups reach this stage and if they do then the group is able to take control of itself. The trainer may feel redundant and may find it difficult to "let go" of the group.

Useful activities: consider yourself as a resource and a facilitator rather than a trainer, be flexible in providing facilities and support when requested to do so.

5 MOURNING

The final stage in the life of a group. This may start a few weeks before the group formally ends. It is marked by exchanges of addresses and phone numbers, arrangements for a farewell party or other ritual mourning process. Participants will need time to say their goodbyes and remember the high and low spots of the learning experience. Some people handle this stage by leaving early or not attending the final session.

Useful activities include: allow time for meaningful goodbyes, allow time for a review of the group life.

Facilitating group development

TEN "MUSTS" THAT INTERFERE WITH GROUP FACILITATION

(Adapted from R. Nelson-Jones, *Lifeskills: a handbook*, Cassell, 1991)

This list presents a set of beliefs that, if held by the trainer, will interfere with group facilitation.

1   I must be the sole source of wisdom in the group.
2   I must be in control of the group at all times.
3   I must be aware of everything that goes on in the group.
4   I must be liked at all times by all participants.
5   I must always maintain a professional façade.
6   I must pressurize participants to self-disclose.
7   I must ensure that great attention is paid to relationship issues between participants.
8   I must always have an explanation or interpretation for everything.
9   Facilitating a training group must be all work and no play.
10 I must always get the balance right between presentation, structured exercise and group discussion.

WORKING WITH CHALLENGING PEOPLE

> There are no difficult learners only inflexible trainers
>
> Anon

All trainers meet up with challenging participants and groups at some stage or other and this may be the result of the participant(s):

- not wanting to attend the course
- having low expectations about the course
- feeling uncomfortable with the trainer
- feeling uncomfortable with one or more participants
- feeling uncomfortable with the environment
- being distracted by factors in the workplace (e.g., forthcoming disciplinary meeting, forthcoming merger, restructuring of department)

- being distracted by factors outside the workplace (e.g., argument with partner, family health problems, debt problems).

Many of these factors have nothing to do with the trainer, but if the trainer does not manage the situation, then they can adversely affect the training event. Alternatively, they can be the result of the group being in the "storming" phase of its development. Siddons (1997) identifies "the frightful four" common difficulties affecting the whole group as:

- one or more participants talking too much and not allowing others to contribute
- several participants not joining in
- participants having side conversations
- disagreement leading to confrontation.

In most groups a few participants are willing to talk and become involved in discussions and this may result in others not contributing. Possible ways of handling this situation include:

- setting up appropriate ground rules at the start of the session
- acknowledging their contribution and asking for someone else's
- acknowledging their contribution and pointing out that everyone needs an opportunity to speak
- structuring discussions and feedback sessions so that everyone has an equal opportunity to speak
- giving them a task, e.g., observing and reporting back, so that they focus on this during a discussion
- letting the group handle it.

This problem is sometimes associated with the formation of cliques. This can have a very detrimental effect on the whole course as other participants may feel like "outsiders." A key strategy is to structure exercises and activities so that the clique members can't work together.

Sometimes one or more people will not join in the course, for example as a result of more senior staff being present, because they feel that they have nothing to contribute, or because they need more time to think. Possible ways of handling this situation include:

- giving them more time
- setting up small group work and ensuring that everyone has an opportunity to feed back
- making eye contact and asking for their views.

There are two main types of side conversations: those that are about the course content and take place through the participants' interest and enthusiasm; and those that have nothing to do with the course and are, perhaps, a sign of boredom. Possible ways of handling this include:

- setting up appropriate ground rules at the start of the session
- stopping talking and waiting for them to be quiet
- asking them to share their conversation with the whole group
- asking them a direct question.

The final common type of challenging situation is when there is a major disagreement between one or more participants and the rest of the group. This can be handled in a number of different ways:

- interrupting the discussion with a direct question and refocusing them on the training materials
- bringing another participant into the discussions
- summarizing the differences stating that everyone is entitled to their own opinion and then moving on to a new topic
- asking everyone to summarize their position with the evidence to support it and then asking them to "agree to disagree" (this has the added value of them actually agreeing about something!)
- changing the subject
- speaking to the people concerned outside the training room.

Above all you must seek to take control immediately, and never take sides.

Siddons (1997) also identifies the problems that can arise with individual participants and these are summarized in Table 10.2 with ways of handling the situation.

Table 10.2   *Challenging individuals (Adapted from S. Siddons, Delivering training, IPD, 1997)*

Challenging behaviors	Possible strategies
The know-it-all	Acknowledge their knowledge and experience and get them to contribute when you want them to (not when they choose to)
	Use them as a second trainer
	Suggest they focus on new ideas/skills rather than on what they already know
	Give them a special role that helps you to manage their interventions
	Provide structured exercises and feedback sessions so that everyone has a turn
	Let the group handle it
	Do not antagonize
People who digress from the topic	Remind everyone of the learning outcomes and bring them back to the topic
	Ask them to hold onto their comments until later, e.g., at the break
People who moan about their manager, team, library	Do not collude by sympathizing or joining in
	Bring the discussion back to the training materials
	Emphasize the purpose of the training event
People who raise personal issues	If relevant then handle it there and then
	If not relevant to the training event then acknowledge it and ask them to raise it with you (or another appropriate person) at the break
People who appear to dislike the trainer	At break time, find out if there is any unresolved conflict
	Do not get involved in an argument
	Work with the person through other group members and use small groups
Persistent lateness	Set up appropriate ground rules at the start of the session
	Start on time
	Discuss with the latecomer, e.g., at a break
People who "put down" other participants	Set up appropriate ground rules at the start of the session
	Remind everyone that "put downs" are unacceptable
	Remind everyone that they all have something different and worthwhile to contribute
	Speak to the person concerned privately
People who ignore/avoid working with others	Set up appropriate ground rules at the start of the session
	Arrange the groups that people work in so that there is a good mix of personalities in each group
	Remind everyone that they all have something different and worthwhile to contribute
	Speak to the person concerned privately

DEALING WITH UNEXPECTED SITUATIONS

This section is concerned with dealing with difficult situations which may affect individual participants or whole groups. These kinds of situations may arise as a result of interruptions, for example participants arriving late, room not being available, or they may be the result of situations which have a greater impact on the participants, learning group and trainer such as:

- bereavement
- accidents
- crime
- change of trainer
- interpersonal conflict.

Strategies for dealing with interruptions

(Adapted from S. Brown, C. Earlam, P. Race, *500 tips for teachers,* Kogan Page, 1995)

1   Accept that there is a disruption.
2   Acknowledge the disruption (either internally and/or externally).
3   Note where you are in your session plan.
4   Deal with the disruption.
5   Have a break if appropriate.
6   Change it into a positive experience (if possible).
7   Signal the continuation of the session.
8   Refocus and start the session.
9   Complete the session.
10   Follow it up later (if appropriate).

EXAMPLES

The following examples have been collected from a number of library trainers.

I didn't expect this to happen . . .

Examples	Strategies for effective action
Two participants arrived ten minutes late.	I acknowledged their arrival in a friendly manner and continued with the session. At an appropriate time I let them get up-to-date with what they had missed. If this was a regular occurrence then I would discuss it with them and negotiate boundaries of behavior.
The whole group arrived five minutes late. They were very excited due to a local fire.	I gave them a chance to settle down. I acknowledged the event. I started with a focusing activity.
There was a bomb scare ten minutes before the end of the session. We immediately evacuated the building. I found out that we would not be able to return to the room for at least an hour. The participants began to go home.	I stayed with the participants and "ended" the class by saying that we would not resume the training event. The next day I contacted everyone by e-mail to "close the session" and obtain course evaluations.
One of the participants had a *grand mal* epileptic attack.	I put her in the recovery position. I then asked everyone to leave the room (to give her privacy) and suggested they go to the restaurant and have a coffee break. One of her colleagues, a first aider, offered to stay with her and look after her needs. I then found an alternative training room. I rejoined the group and explained what was

happening. We then reconvened the group session. I acknowledged what had happened and then moved on to a focusing activity. Once the group got going, I followed up what was happening with the participant who had been taken ill. I arranged for a taxi and her colleague offered to accompany her home.

In a library skills course at a university one of the students appeared unable to understand what I was saying and I noticed that his pupils were dilated. His breathing seemed strange. I suspected a drugs incident.	I put him in the recovery position. I asked one student to go to the library reception desk and ask them to dial 911 and ask for an ambulance. I explained the symptoms that they needed to tell the ambulance service. I asked him to ask reception to send a member of library staff to help me. I asked the other students to have a 20-minute break. I asked two students (who lived in the same house) to stay with us. When my colleague arrived I asked her to contact the university health and safety officer, phone the traffic control office and tell them to expect an ambulance, and to inform the Faculty Office. The ambulance arrived within ten minutes and took the student with one of his friends to the hospital. I then had a cup of coffee and began completing the formal "incident" reporting procedures. I was supported by my colleague and the university health and safety officer. I then restarted the session.
A workshop in a public library one of the participants brought his two seven-year-old twins with him. They began to mess about and disturb other learners.	I explained to the parent that there was a problem with the presence of the children in the workshop – I was concerned about the children both from a health and safety point of view and the effect that they were having on other learners. I suggested that he come back and complete the workshop when they were at school and explained that he would get more out of it if he wasn't distracted. After a few complaints about the lack of daycare facilities (which I agreed with) he went. He did return to the next workshop without the twins. In retrospect I think we should have advertised it differently and made it clear from the start that children couldn't attend the workshop.

Checklist for managing emotional learners

(Adapted from S. Brown, C. Earlam, P. Race, *500 tips for teachers,* Kogan Page, 1995)

1 Accept the emotion. Asking anyone to "pull themselves together" or "snap out of it" is unhelpful.
2 Find out what's behind the emotion. This is sometimes best carried out in privacy and it may take some time to find the real cause rather than the "presenting" cause.
3 Encourage the learner to put his/her experience into his/her own words. This is often the starting point to resolving the situation.
4 Avoid alienating the person affected by the emotion. Help them to feel that a range of emotions is a normal response to particular situations and that there is no shame attached to displaying emotions.

5   Help the learner to identify the source of their emotion. Often by articulating how and why we feel something the feelings become more manageable.

6   Get help and support.

7   If you are working within an educational context then your organization is likely to have trained counsellors or pastoral support workers who can help out in difficult situations. It is worthwhile making contact with them before you need to use their services. Colleagues often have a vast store of experience of managing difficult situations and it is helpful to be aware of their resources too.

8   If you are working in other sectors then the human resource service may include a counselling service. This is sometimes contracted out to an independent body. It is worthwhile making contact with them before you need to use their services. Colleagues often have a vast store of experience of managing difficult situations and it is helpful to be aware of their resources too.

9   Follow up. Follow up the particular incident or event to ensure that it has been resolved and that the learner(s) and yourself are receiving the support you need.

LEARNING TRANSFER

Transfer of learning refers to the successful application of knowledge and skills learned during a training process in the library. If learning transfer does not take place then the training process has been ineffective and very wasteful. Research on learning transfer, e.g., Broad and Newstrom (1992), suggests that only 40% of the material is transferred immediately after the event, 25% still applied six months later and only 15% twelve months after the training event.

The approach to training described in this book is designed to produce high levels of learning transfer. The following checklist highlights particular ways of enhancing transfer.

10+ ways to help transfer learning into the workplace

1   Identify work-based goals at the start of the course.

2   Make the sessions interesting and relevant and use accelerated learning techniques.

3   Provide clear and detailed course materials.

4   Include practice sessions to ensure that the learners are confident about applying their new skills to the workplace.

5   Provide feedback so that the learners know what they have learned.

6   Provide opportunities for asking questions.

7   Provide or develop resources for use in the workplace.

8 Provide opportunities for integrating and synthesizing learning, e.g., through the use of visual tools such as mind maps.

9 Set time aside for discussing implementation in the workplace.

10 Establish a buddy system to enable participants to support each other back in the workplace.

11 Organize postcourse support groups, e.g., by phone, e-mail or meetings.

12 Organize a follow-up session, e.g., three months after the training event.

13 Include action planning toward the end of the course. This is described in detail in Chapter 9 where there are two sample action plan forms.

ENDING GROUP SESSIONS

Toward the end of the session, the trainer needs to ensure that:

- the formal learning processes are completed for that day
- the forthcoming ending of the session is signalled
- learners are prepared for moving back into their environments, e.g., work, travel, home life or caring for others.

In this section, we introduce a range of approaches for ending learning sessions. We also look at some of the difficulties that may arise at these times and approaches to overcoming them.

The ending of a learning session needs careful management to make sure that when it occurs:

- the learning process is consolidated
- there is time for reflection (see Chapter 4)
- the group process is completed
- individuals have a sense of reaching an ending and they have no unfinished business
- individuals are prepared to move on to another environment
- the next stage is signalled
- the training event is evaluated (this is considered in the next chapter)
- there is time to complete the closing process in an unhurried way.

Ideally, the session should end on a positive note with the trainer's closing comments genuinely summarizing the event and the students' learning achievements.

5 ways of acknowledging the learning that has taken place

1 Ask participants to form groups and create a mind map (see pp. 168–9) of their learning from the course.

2 Hold a final quiz.

3 Have presentations or reports from individuals or groups.

4 Summarize, e.g., with a metaphor, the journey which has been travelled by the group.

5 Organize a mini review.

9 ways to close a session

(Adapted from B. Hopson and M. Scally, *Lifeskills teaching*, McGraw-Hill, 1981)

1 CELEBRATE LEARNING

Participants need to be given the opportunity to focus on what they have gained from the learning session. This could be achieved by asking them to summarize or review the material, individually, in pairs or small groups. It could be structured to cover what they learned and also how they learned it. This could result in a set of personal notes, sharing ideas via a flipchart or a mind map. There could be a round in which everyone (including the trainer) states their most significant learning from the session.

2 ENSURE MEANING

Provide an opportunity for participants to identify how they will apply their new knowledge or skills to their working lives, for example ask them to identify one thing that they will do differently as a result of the training event, ask them to write this down and share it with two colleagues. The purpose behind the activity of writing it down and sharing with a colleague is to embed the action and make it more likely to happen.

3 ACTION PLANS

Individual participants, trainer and group action plans need to be clearly identified so that everyone knows who is responsible for following up different actions. Two example action plans are presented in Chapter 9.

4 FUTURE SESSIONS

The details of the next session (if there is going to be one) and any preparation that needs to be carried out for it need to be announced to the participants.

5 DEALING WITH UNFINISHED BUSINESS

Any "unfinished business," for example issues or feelings raised and not followed up, needs to be acknowledged with an indication of when and how it will be dealt with.

6 FEEDBACK AND EVALUATION

Participants need some time to comment on and give their responses to the session. This may be handled by an open forum. Guidance may be given in the form "Say one thing that you have enjoyed about today's session and one change that you would like to see in future sessions." It can be handled by asking participants to write their comments on post-it notes and to stick them on the board before they go. Formal evaluation forms also give them the opportunity to feed back their responses to the event. The subject of evaluation is considered in the next chapter.

7 APPOINTMENTS

If the participants have to work in pairs or small groups before the next formal session then they will need time to make appointments with one another.

8 PREPARING TO MOVE ON

Participants will need time to refocus and prepare themselves for their next activity.

9 FINAL SIGNAL

The trainer needs to formally signal the end of the session: "We have finished for today."

5 ways of eliciting a feeling of completion

1 Use a closing ritual
2 Hold a celebration, give certificates, awards, handshakes
3 Have a party
4 Hold a mock awards ceremony, e.g., the participant with the loudest laugh, etc.
5 Make a farewell speech or tell a story.

5+ ways of saying "good-bye"

1 Tell a story.
2 Make a mini speech.
3 Hold a poster session where everyone has the opportunity to give written positive feedback to everyone else in the group.
4 Use a symbolic dance or ritual.
5 Have a meal or coffee and pastry.
6 Have a round in which everyone says good-bye and identifies what they will take from the training event.

Unexpected endings

Sometimes training sessions end unexpectedly or with unexpected events. Below are a few examples of situations that could arise.

EXAMPLE

1 It is two hours before the end of a one-day training event. One of the participants declares "I hate this course. It's useless. I'm leaving." The other participants look upset, embarrassed or annoyed.

2 It is the final session of a training event. The participants are all getting ready to leave. You are in the middle of good-byes. The fire bell goes off. The college kitchen is on fire. You all have to evacuate the building. Half an hour later the building is still evacuated and most of your group has disappeared. A few participants from the group are still there. There is a feeling of unfinished business.

3 You are coming to the end of the learning session and it appears to have been a positive and productive session. Suddenly an argument erupts between two participants – they seem to be fighting over a letter. The atmosphere disintegrates and becomes tense and aggressive.

4 The training event has ended and one of the participants comes up to you and asks to talk with you. She has looked upset throughout the day. She bursts into tears and says that her mother is seriously ill. You have a meeting in 15 minutes.

How do you handle each of these situations? There is no perfect answer! You need to work out your own response giving thought to:

- the needs of the individual
- the needs of the whole group
- your own needs.

11
Evaluating training sessions

INTRODUCTION

This chapter is concerned with evaluating training and the outcomes of training to ensure that they meet the changing needs of the library. Hackett (1997) summarizes it as follows:

> Evaluation is about trying to assess whether or not training is indeed producing relevant and valued outputs through efficient and well-managed processes. It is itself a process – of gathering information with which to make decisions about training activities.

In this chapter we will look at the following topics:

- purpose of evaluation
- approaches to evaluation
- tools for evaluation
- results of evaluation.

PURPOSE OF EVALUATION

Evaluation has three main purposes:

- to ensure that the training practice is aligned with library objectives
- to provide feedback about the running of the program
- to provide feedback to trainers so that they can improve their program(s).

APPROACHES TO EVALUATION

A structured approach to the evaluation process helps to ensure that you achieve its aims and objectives. One framework for the evaluation process is described below.

Twenty questions about the evaluation process

(From Open University, *Planning, monitoring and evaluating learning programs,* People and potential, Study Unit 3, 1994)

PLANNING EVALUATION

1 Why is the evaluation to be carried out?
2 What outcomes are to be evaluated?
3 How will the evaluation be conducted?

DESIGNING THE PROCESS

4 What criteria will be used to make judgments?
5 Who will undertake evaluation?
6 What resources will be available?
7 What records need to be established for monitoring purposes?

CONDUCTING EVALUATION

8 What type(s) of information will be collected?
9 How will information be collected – through records, questioning, observation, reading?
10 How will the results be sorted for analysis?

PRESENTING EVALUATION

11 Who will write the report?
12 Who is the report for?
13 What level of interpretation and recommendations will it include?
14 Who will receive the report?

ASSESSING EVALUATION

15 Who will judge success?
16 Who will recommend change?

APPLICATION OF FINDINGS

17 Who will be responsible for changes to the plans for the next learning event/program?
18 Who will be responsible for changes to the practice of delivering programs?

REVIEW OF EVALUATION PROCESS

19 Who will review the evaluation process?

20 Who will redesign the evaluation process (if needed)?

There are two main approaches to evaluation: evaluating the running of a training program and evaluating the event itself. These are considered in turn.

EVALUATING THE RUNNING OF A TRAINING PROGRAM

Bramley (1996) provides a useful checklist of questions which can be used to evaluate the process for a particular training program:

TARGET POPULATION

1 Are the right people coming to the program?

2 Are they coming at the right time?

3 Are they being briefed properly before they come?

4 What proportion of attendees attend the program for such reasons as: a rest, his/her turn for training, someone else dropped out?

OBJECTIVES

5 What changes are expected to result from the program in terms of:
   – individual performance levels?
   – organizational effectiveness?

6 Are the objectives clear and unambiguous?

7 Do the trainers know the participant's individual learning objectives? How are they taking these into account?

COURSE STRUCTURE

8 On what learning principles is the course structured?

9 Is there a satisfactory balance between practice, reflection and theoretical input?

10 Is the program the right length?

11 Does the balance of the course reflect the different degrees of importance attached to the objectives?

METHODS AND MEDIA

12 On what basis have the methods been chosen?

13 Are behavioral methods used when behavioral change is expected?

14 Are mental maps being built up where problem solving is expected?

15 Are the characteristics of the learners considered?

16 Do the methods and media provide variety and encourage learning?

17 What are the quality and reliability of handouts, computer-based training material and training aids?

EVALUATIVE FEEDBACK

18 How is progress being assessed during the program?

19 Is each assessment method reliable and timely?

20 How is feedback given to the participants?

21 How is feedback used by the trainers? Is there enough flexibility to allow for its use?

EVALUATING THE TRAINING EVENT

Evaluation of the training event is likely to take place at a number of different levels:

- reaction
- learning
- changes in behavior
- impact of change on library.

These different levels of evaluation are explored in detail in this section.

The reaction to the training is how people feel when they leave the training event. This is their immediate response without time to reflect on the event or apply their learning in the workplace. The next level of evaluation is concerned with what knowledge or skills someone has learned as a result of the training event. What impact has the training activity had on the participant's behavior in the workplace? The final level of evaluation is the impact on the library.

Different people may be involved in the evaluation process, for example participants, trainers, workplace colleagues, team leaders and managers. Involving a number of different people obviously improves the quality of the evaluation process and it also increases the cost (in both time and other resources).

Some evaluation processes measure the impact of the training across time and this may result in the type of evaluation process described in the following example.

EXAMPLE

Performance appraisal training program: evaluation process

	Time	Evaluation activity
1	Day of training event	Measure reaction to training event through evaluation form
2	One month later	Measure learning through evaluation form to participant

3	Three months later (after first round of performance management meetings)	Measure behavior through evaluation form to appraisees (participants) and appraisers (team leaders)
		Measure behavior by monitoring completed appraisal forms
4	Twelve months later (after first round of performance management process)	Measure behavior through evaluation form to appraisees (participants) and appraisers (team leaders)
		Measure behavior by monitoring completed appraisal forms
		Measure impact on library by monitoring performance indicators, annual customer service survey, evaluation form to Heads of Service

The example above shows the use of questionnaires, monitoring workplace documents, and performance indicators and surveys as tools for evaluation. There are a wide range of tools available and these are described in Table 11.1.

Table 11.1 *Tools for evaluation* (Adapted from P. Hackett, *Introduction to training*, IPD, 1997)

	Reactions	Learning	Behavior	Impact on library
Participant questionnaires or reports	•	•	•	•
Manager questionnaires or reports	•	•	•	•
Written test		•		
Practical test or demonstration		•	•	
Customer survey			•	•
Employer survey			•	•
Interviews	•	•	•	•
Performance appraisal		•	•	
Observation		•	•	
Impact on library performance indicators				•
Impact on team/unit indicators				•
Impact on personal performance indicators				•
Top management opinion	•	•	•	•
Recognition as investors in people				•

Evaluating the reaction

This is probably the most common form of evaluation that takes place during training events and it provides information about the reaction of the participants to the training event.

FIVE WAYS TO EVALUATE THE REACTIONS TO A SESSION

1 Ask individual participants to write on a post-it note their key learning from the course and one change that they would like the trainer to make the next time he/she runs the session.
2 Ask individual participants to fill in a questionnaire.
3 Have a round and ask everyone to identify their main learning from the course and one thing that they would like to be done differently.

4   Ask participants to write a brief (no more than 50 words) metaphor about the training event.

5   In groups ask participants to identify what they liked about the course/what they didn't like/what they learned/what they would like changed. Ask them to write up their findings on a flipchart and share them with the whole group.

EXAMPLE REACTION STATEMENTS

(From A. Kirby, *Games for trainers* 3, Gower, 1994)

Please complete the following reaction statements in whatever way is most appropriate for you.

This course made me feel . . .
I liked . . .
I was surprised by . . .
I'll use . . .
Now I can . . .
I didn't like . . .
I wish we'd had time to . . .
I want to know more about . . .
The next thing I have to do is . . .
I'd also like to say . . .

This type of feedback provides some useful general information.

Obtaining more detailed information is more helpful in terms of providing guidance on where improvements can be made to the training events. Very specific questions can be included, as demonstrated below.

EXAMPLE

This is the first time we have used the cataloging procedures exercise (blue sheets). Please would you comment on this particular exercise. What did you learn from it?

Please comment on the open learning package (Introduction to Word). You can comment using the following headings:

Structure and organization

Exercises and activities

Visual appearance

Language

Any other comments

Library: Staff development evaluation form

We are always actively seeking to improve the standard of our training. Please help us to assess the value of this session by completing this questionnaire.

Title of course:
Trainer:
Venue: **Date**:

Please check a box to indicate your rating of each factor.
1 = very poor, 2 = poor, 3 = satisfactory, 4 = good, 5 = excellent

	1	2	3	4	5
Was the event					
Interesting?					
Useful?					
Easy to understand?					
Paced appropriately?					
Did the event					
Enable you to participate?					
Provide a variety of learning activities?					
Were the learning materials					
Clear?					
Well presented?					
Useful?					
Were the trainers					
Well prepared?					
Enthusiastic?					
Responsive to your learning needs?					
Housekeeping details					
Please rate the training room					
Please rate the catering					

If the event did not meet your expectations, please explain why

What were the best things about the event?

What aspects of the event (if any) would you change for the future?

Thank you for completing this form. Please hand it to your trainer.

Figure 11.1   *Sample evaluation form*

Evaluating the learning

KNOWLEDGE

How do you evaluate the learning that has taken place? Bramley (1996) identifies three levels of evaluation:

- Level 1. "Facts." This can be carried out by asking the participants open-ended short answer questions, e.g., in the form of tests or quizzes.
- Level 2. "Procedures." This can also be tested using open-ended short answer questions and asking "what comes next?" or "what would you do if . . . ?" types of questions.
- Level 3. "Analysis." This can be evaluated by asking the learners to respond to complex examples, e.g., mini scenarios or case studies.

In library training sessions formal evaluation of knowledge takes place when the training event is part of a learning program leading to a degree. Informal evaluation may take place toward the end of a training event through the use of question sheets, quizzes, or games. These can have a powerful effect on the participants as they help them to integrate their learning and also show them how much they know, which can be a powerful motivator.

SKILLS

Evaluation of learning or development of skills can be carried out at the end of a training session by asking someone to demonstrate the skill. In the library, the team leader or manager can evaluate the skill by observing the member of staff practicing it.

The library trainer may want to observe someone demonstrating his/her skills as part of the training program. Alternatively they may like to send a form to the participant and his/her leader to ask for a work-based assessment.

Changes in behavior at work

Evaluating changes in behavior at work is a more challenging activity as it involves collecting evidence about knowledge, skills, behavior, feelings, beliefs and values.

One approach to this type of evaluation process is described by Bramley (1996), who suggests that a starting point is to think about behavior change as moving people along a continuum. Start with where they are on the line. This is shown in Figure 11.2.

aware of proposed methods	evaluation no longer negative	willing to try new methods	preference for new methods	identification with new methods	incorporation into new routines

Figure 11.2 *The behaviour change continuum*

One method of assessing this development process is by assessing self-confidence with respect to a particular task or activity and this is shown in Figure 11.3.

Evaluation of MS Project training program		
Task	Can do yes/no	If yes, confidence on a scale of 1–10 (10 high)
Start/quit Project 98		
Open/close/create/save/ project file		
Create/use a project template		
Use the following views: Gantt chart, PERT chart, Calendar view		
Define and manage tasks		
Define and assign resources		
Work with costs and workload		
Progress a project, tasks, resources, costs and workloads		
Printing a project, reports		

Figure 11.3 *Sample evaluation form assessing learner's self-confidence*

Evaluating the impact on the library

This is the hardest type of evaluation process and possibly the most important. The actual method used will depend on the nature of the library goals and the factors it has identified as critical to successful performance.

This is a very specialized area and in-depth knowledge of survey techniques and quantitative methods is required. There are software tools available that will help library staff with this process. Many libraries carry out regular user surveys and these offer an approach to evaluating the impact on the library. Direct correlation between training and library performance is difficult to demonstrate.

EXAMPLE

A liberal arts college includes the following questions in its annual student survey:

Library and Learning Resource Staff	poor	satisfactory	good	excellent
Are staff efficient in dealing with inquiries?				
How are the answers which staff give to inquiries rated?				

It is difficult to link the findings from this survey with the training program on reference skills because the questions are so general.

Other information and library services provide more in-depth questions about their staff. The example in Figure 11.4 comes from a university library service and provides a more detailed analysis of customer services. This provides more information to work with, but it is important to remember that a whole range of variables are operating so that it is still difficult to identify the impact of the training program.

RESULTS OF EVALUATION

The findings from the evaluation process may result in a number of different outcomes:

- the training is abandoned
- the training is redesigned – new learning objectives, new structure, new content, new methods, new trainer
- the preparation work is redesigned – new briefing material, new pre-course work
- the training process is changed – new selection method, new timing, no change.

Library staff	Yes/no	If yes then please score from 1–5 (1=low, 5=high)
Reference staff		
Are staff approachable?		
Are staff helpful?		
Are staff efficient in dealing with reference queries?		
Do you obtain relevant answers to reference queries?		
Do you obtain correct answers to your reference queries?		
Any comments		
IT staff		
Are staff approachable?		
Are staff helpful?		
Are staff efficient in dealing with IT queries?		
Do you obtain relevant answers to your IT queries?		
Do you obtain correct answers to your IT queries?		
Any comments		
AV/media staff		
Are staff approachable?		
Are staff helpful?		
Are staff efficient in dealing with AV/media queries?		
Do you obtain relevant answers to your AV/media queries?		
Do you obtain correct answers to your AV/media queries?		
Any comments		
Information desk staff		
Are staff approachable?		
Are staff helpful?		
Are staff efficient in dealing with your issues/returns?		
Are staff efficient in dealing with your reservations?		
Any comments		

Figure 11.4 *Customer service questionnaire*

Part 3

Professional development for library trainers

12
Continuing professional development

INTRODUCTION

Continuous professional development enables all library professionals to learn and develop so that they update their existing knowledge and skills, and also develop new knowledge and skills. The development of training skills is a continuous process and it may involve the following types of learning processes:

- learning through training practice
- learning through other activities
- learning through training programs.

LEARNING THROUGH TRAINING PRACTICE

A key development route is through practice and reflection on training activities. The following activities provide examples of some of the ways in which individual trainers can develop their skills.

12 activities for learning through training practice

1 ACCELERATED LEARNING

The next time you run a training session choose one of the ideas from the checklist 15+ ideas for using multisensory approaches to learning (pp. 15–20). Try out this idea. Reflect on your findings using the following format:

- event: title, date
- what happened
- what I have learned
- action(s).

2 AUDIOTAPING

Audiotaping is a useful way of obtaining feedback about your training sessions. It can be carried out discreetly and is a relatively unobtrusive activity. Remember to obtain permission from the course members. The only equipment that you need is a tape recorder and blank tape. Tape the whole session or part of it. In practice, you may find tapes that are over an hour long too time-consuming to listen to afterward. Listen to the tape – either in private or with a colleague. Identify at least one development activity for yourself.

3 COTRAINERS

Explore the possibility of cotraining on a future event. If you decide to cotrain then complete an action plan (see Chapter 9) to support you through that process. Follow the guidelines presented on pp. 152–4. Reflect on the results.

4 FEEDBACK

This is probably the most important source of learning in the workplace and is essential for the development of trainers. Trainers can obtain feedback from:

- course members
- cotrainers
- course organizers
- course sponsors.

Feedback from course members can be quickly obtained at the end of each session. A simple method of obtaining useful feedback is to ask each course member to write down:

- the most important thing they learned from the course
- one thing that they would like the trainer to do differently next time he/she runs the course.

These answers can be collected on post-it notes.

Feedback from cotrainers, course organizers or course sponsors may be obtained by asking specific questions such as:

- What worked best?
- What could be changed next time?
- Were there any irritations during the program/run-up to the program?
- What feedback have you obtained from participants?

5 LEARNING LOG

A learning log is a simple tool for recording, developing and structuring learning experiences. A particular incident or experience may be used as the focus for a learning log entry which may be structured as follows:

- event
- what happened (description in less than 50 words)
- what I have learned
- what I will do differently next time.

Figure 12.1 shows a sample page from the learning log of a library IT skills trainer.

---

1   *Learning to use the Internet. 12.10.99*

2   *Examples*

    a) Jane got left behind in practical exercises and she got upset.

    b) I couldn't answer question about HTML detail.

3   *My learning*

    a) I need to change the way I set up exercises. Change
       instructions? Develop a self-learning package?

    b) I need to learn more about HTML.

4   *Actions*

    a) Discuss Jane scenario with John on Tuesday (10 am) and
       decide what to do for next course.

    b) Book myself on next HTML course. Make phone call today!

Figure 12.1   *Sample page from a learning log*

6 LEARNING STYLES

Review one of your own training sessions. Assess your own use of the 4MAT approach (see pp. 128–31). What learning styles did you match? Were any left out? How do your findings relate to your own learning preferences?

7 OBSERVATION

This is an important and potentially sensitive form of staff development. Invite a colleague or another trainer into your training session as a silent observer. Identify the areas where you want to receive feedback before the session. At the end of the session ask them to provide you with feedback. You may want to structure your feedback in a formal manner. An example observation sheet is presented in Figure 12.2.

Trainer – please highlight the specific areas (no more than three) on which you want to receive feedback.

Features	Comments
Physical environment	
Organization of presenter	
Start of presentation	
Attention grabber	
Introductions	
Clear objectives/learning outcomes	
End of presentation	
Clearly signposted/guided	
Energetic	
Reinforcement of the key message(s)	
Audience left on a positive note	
Clear ending	
Structure	
Clear beginning, middle, end	
Little what, why, what, how, what if?	
Signposts, summaries and linking statements	
Content	
Level of knowledge	
Logical ordering of subject	
Relevant	
Appropriate examples	
Appropriate level of content	
Presentation techniques	
Use of visual aids/examples	
Use of auditory aids/examples	
Use of kinesthetic aids/examples	
Humor	
Use of stories/anecdotes and metaphors	
Spatial anchors	
Use of different activities	
Use of Satir techniques	
Use of handouts	
Use of IT	
Use of demonstrations	
Use of questions	
Use of discussion	
Time for feedback from group	
Presenter	
Well organized	
Eye contact	
Rapport with group	
Presentation of self	
Energy levels	
Use of voice – tone, etc.	
Interest in subject	
Enthusiasm	
Movement	

Figure 12.2   *Sample observation form*

8 PLANNING TRAINING EVENTS

Next time you plan a training event do it differently, for example if you always plan them by yourself then ask a colleague to work with you, if you always plan training events with a particular colleague then ask someone different to work with you. Notice the differences and reflect on them.

9 RUNNING LEARNING GROUPS

Look at the ideas presented in Chapter 10. Choose one (relevant and appropriate) idea that you haven't applied in a training context. Implement the idea. Notice the impact. Reflect on your findings.

10 TRAINING METHODS

Feedback to some trainers suggests that they tend to use tried and tested methods and rarely try new ones. The next time you plan and run a training event then incorporate a new training method. Obviously it will have to fit your training outcomes and planning considerations. Notice the impact of the method. Ask the participants for feedback at the end. Reflect on your findings.

11 TRAINING SKILLS

There are many ideas contained in Chapter 4. Choose one area you want to develop. You may want to ask a colleague for help in identifying an area for development. Identify an action plan. Put it into action and then obtain feedback. Then move on to another area for development.

EXAMPLE

An information officer wanted to develop her skills in motivating others. She liked the idea of metaprograms (see Tables 4.3 to 4.7) but found them rather overwhelming. She decided to learn more about the metaprograms and how they could be used on courses. This is her action plan.

a   Read a book on metaprograms.

b   Search the Internet and obtain more information about them.

c   Each week choose one metaprogram and see if I can identify my colleagues' preferences in the workplace. Make notes on my findings.

d   Discuss my findings with my son [a psychology student].

e   Identify three ways in which I can use metaprograms on the "Advanced information systems" program I am running next month.

12 VIDEO

Videoing ourselves training is a useful way of obtaining feedback. It has the disadvantage of being a fairly intrusive activity and occasionally a course member will not give permission to be videoed. Some people find videoing off-putting and may behave in an unnatural manner.

Video cameras are required and must be set up in advance. The video can be played back either in private or with trusted colleagues. This then provides an opportunity to acknowledge strengths and identify areas for development.

LEARNING THROUGH OTHER ACTIVITIES

There are many other approaches to developing training skills which involve other work-based learning activities. A number of examples are given in the following section.

5+ approaches to learning through other activities

ASSISTING ANOTHER TRAINER

Chapter 3 describes the role of training assistants, i.e., people who act as voluntary helpers or support staff to a trainer. Assisting offers a number of different development opportunities as it gives you the opportunity to:

- learn how another trainer works (and have an opportunity to discuss their specific strategies with them outside of the actual training event)
- review a training event and training material
- observe group dynamics and processes.

COMPUTER-MEDIATED COMMUNICATIONS

Computer-mediated communications (CMC) are becoming increasingly significant as a development tool. CMC is an umbrella term which includes:

- electronic mail
- electronic discussion groups
- electronic bulletin boards
- computer conferencing systems
- groupware
- Internet applications.

CMC offers the following options:

- access to information
- exchange of information

- exchange of data files
- research facilities (e.g., to disseminate questionnaires)
- access to online learning resources and programs
- access to online tutoring
- access to open and closed discussion groups (in-house, national, international)
- access to professional colleagues, e.g., at regional, national and international levels
- access to other professional colleagues, e.g., trainers in other sectors.

There are an increasing number of online information and discussion groups available both within the library profession and externally. For example, the American Society for Training and Development (www. astd.org) has a "live chat" which can provide useful information on training.

CONFERENCES

Conferences provide a useful means of networking and exchanging information and ideas. There are many excellent conferences organized each year. Specialist conferences on training and facilitating learning are held by many organizations and groups. Attending conferences organized by other professional groups, for example human resource professionals or learning professionals (such as groups concerned with distance learning or NLP) offer an opportunity to exchange ideas with professional staff who are working in a different context.

EXHIBITS

Exhibits offer an opportunity to identify new learning resources and techniques. Walking around booths looking at books, learning packages, videos and presentations provides a wealth of new resources and ideas.

If you attend an exhibit then you are likely to gain more from it if you set yourself some specific objectives at the start of the day.

EXAMPLE

I attended a training and development exhibit in Chicago. My objectives were to:

- identify a computer software package which could be used for mind mapping
- identify a new set of resources on team building
- identify a book of new icebreakers.

I found that these objectives helped me to focus my day. I achieved them.

MENTORING

Mentoring is described in Chapter 3. Working with a mentor offers new approaches to thinking and working with training events. Mentors are often a useful source of new ideas, contacts and opportunities.

OBSERVING ANOTHER TRAINER

Attending the training sessions of excellent trainers provides another means of developing training skills. It is worthwhile taking a notebook to record exactly how they train. How do they present information? What methods do they use? Are their sessions structured to take into account the needs of reflectors, theorists, activists, pragmatists? What language do they use? Do their methods and language match the needs of visual, auditory and kinesthetic learners? How many of Howard Gardner's multiple intelligences do they involve? What conclusions have you come to about the trainers' own learning preferences?

PROFESSIONAL ORGANIZATIONS

Professional organizations such as The American Library Association and the American Society for Training and Development provide access to up-to-date information, publications, journals, examples of good practice and meetings. Professional meetings are held throughout the country and offer good opportunities to update ideas, exchange good practice and network.

Membership of organizations outside the library profession, for example the Society for Human Resource Management or the American Society for Training and Development provide access to different perspectives, different groups and activities.

READING

There are many excellent books on accelerated learning and effective training. The resources section in Appendix A provides some guidance.

FINALLY

This book offers all the building blocks that are needed for library staff to provide excellent library training events. Practice and continuous development of these skills will enable library trainers to provide training events in which all their participants:

- enjoy the training event
- learn faster and more effectively
- transfer their skills and ideas into the workplace
- are motivated to learn more about the subject.

As library trainers it is easy to develop and continuously improve as listening and responding to the feedback from our course participants provides vital information which literally feeds that growth process. In addition, the ideas, processes and programs summarized in Part 3 all offer additional pathways for development.

This book provides a trainer's toolbox: a range of ideas, techniques and different approaches to training. Its reflective reading sections offer in themselves a learning opportunity. It is up to individual readers to decide what they are going to take from the book and how they are going to apply the techniques and skills in their library training practice. A comment from a colleague about her personal development as a library trainer is very relevant at this point:

> I now feel that I have a toolbox of skills, methods and techniques. I know that I will use many of them. Some of them I won't use because they don't fit my personal training style. I know that I will be able to keep adding new ideas, exercises and activities into my toolbox. I've become a reflective trainer who will continue to grow.

Enjoy your work in the world of library training and development. Excellent training practice can lead to excellent information and library services.

Appendix: Resources

SAMPLE TRAINING RESOURCES

Allan, B. (1997) *Running learning groups*, Folens.

Burrington, G. (1999) *Understanding disability: a two-day training package for the Library and Information Sector*, Burrington Partnership Publishing.

Hollands, W. D., and Bradley, P. (1999) *Teaching the Internet to library staff and users: 11 ready-to-run workshops that work*, Library Association Publishing.

Honey, P. (1995) *Manual of self-assessment questionnaires*, Peter Honey.

Honey, P., and Mumford, A. (1995) *Manual of learning styles*, Peter Honey.

Jones, K. (1991) *Icebreakers: a source book of games, exercise and simulations*, Kogan Page.

Kirby, A. (1992) *Games for Trainers 1*, Gower.

Kirby, A. (1992) *Games for Trainers 2*, Gower.

Kirby, A. (1994) *Games for Trainers 3*, Gower.

Library Association (1999) *Presentation skills for library and information professionals*, Library Association.

McNamara, D., and Core, J. (1998) *The EduLib Project and its teaching materials*, University of Hull.

Parkin, M. (1998) *Tales for trainers: using stories and metaphors to facilitate learning*, Kogan Page.

Sugar, S. (1998) *Games that teach*, Jossey-Bass/Pfeiffer.

Trotta, M. (1999) *Successful staff development: a how-to-do-it manual*, Neal-Schuman.

Willis, L., and Daisley, J. (1990) *Springboard: women's development workbook*, Hawthorn Press.

ORGANIZATIONS

American Library Association
50 E. Huron St.
Chicago, IL 60611
www.ala.org

American Society for Information Science and Technology
1320 Fenwick Lane, Suite 510
Silver Spring, MD 20910
www.asis.org

American Society for Training and Development
1640 King St., Box 1443
Alexandria, VA 22313

Association for Neuro-Linguistic Programming (ANLP)
P.O. Box 5
Haverford West
Wales SA63 4YA
www.anlp.org

Society for Human Resource Management
1800 Duke St.
Alexandria, VA 22314
www.shrm.org

Special Libraries Association
1700 Eighteenth St., NW
Washington, DC 20009-2514
www.sla.org

REFERENCES

Allan, B. (1997) *Running learning groups*, Folens.

Allan, B. (1998) *Developing learning organizations*, Pitman.

Allan, B. (1999) *Developing information and library staff through work-based learning: 101 activities*, Library Association Publishing.

Allan, B., Cook, M., and Lewis, R. (1996) *Developing independence in learning*, Hull.

Allan, B., and Lewis, D. (1999) *Programme Planning Unit*, Hull.

Allan, B., and Reveley, S. (1999) *Developing training skills in learning support staff, personnel training and education*, **17** (2), 7–10.

Allen, R. E., and Allen, S. D. (1998) *Winnie-the-Pooh on success*, Methuen.

BAC (1979) *Counselling*, BAC.

Ball, C. (1991) *Learning pays: the role of post-compulsory education and training*, Royal Society of Arts.

Barry, C. (1997) Information skills for an electronic world: training doctoral research students, *Journal of Information Science*, **23** (3), 225–38.

Bee, F., and R. (1998) *Facilitation skills*, IPD.

Beel, C., et al. (1995) *Successful strategies: A handbook for trainers and educators*, CCDU.

Bentley, T. (1996) *Sharpen your team's skills in creativity*, McGraw-Hill.

Biddescombe, R. (1996) *Training for IT*, Library Association Publishing.

Black, K. (1996) *Project management for library and information professionals*, Aslib.

de Bono, E. (1992) *Six thinking hats*, Little, Brown and Co.

Bramley, P. (1996) *Evaluating training*, IPD.

Broad, M., and Newstrom, J. W. (1992) *Transfer of training*, Addison-Wesley.

Brown, S., Earlam, C., and Race, P. (1995) *500 tips for teachers*, Kogan Page.

Burden, K., et al. (1995) *Learning to learn: teacher's pack*, Center for Learning.

Burnard, P. (1989) *Counselling skills for health professionals*, Chapman & Hall.

Burnard, P. (1991) Teachers and counsellors, *Employee Counselling Today*, **3** (1), 21–3.

Buzan, T. (1989) *Using both sides of the brain*, Penguin.

Charvet, S. R. (1996) *Words that change minds*, Kendall/Hunt.

Chitty, J., and Muller, M. L. (1990) *Energy exercises*, Polarity Press.

Chopra, D. (1993) *Ageless body, timeless mind*, Rider.

Cook, M. J. (1994) *Effective coaching*, McGraw-Hill.

Dearing Report *see* National Committee for Enquiry into Higher Education.

Delors, J., et al. (1996) *Learning: the treasure within. Report to UNESCO of the International Commission on Education for the Twenty-first Century*, presided over by Jacques Delors, HMSO.

Dennison, P. E., and Dennison, G. E. (1994) *Brain gym: teacher's edition*, Edu-Kinesthetics.

Egan, G. (1990) *The skilled helper*, 4th ed, Brooks/Cole.

Evans, C. (1996) Playing the game, *Library Association Record*, **98** (8), 425.

Fisher, B. (1994) *Mentoring*, Library Association Publishing.

Fryer, R. H. (1997) *Learning for the twenty-first century. First report of the National Advisory Group for Continuing Education and Lifelong Learning*, HMSO.

Garratt, T. (1997) *The effective delivery of training using NLP*, Kogan Page.

Garrett, H., and Taylor, J. (1993) *How to deliver equal opportunities training*, Kogan Page.

Goleman, D. (1996) *Emotional intelligence*, Bloomsbury.

Gough, J. (1996) *Developing learning materials*, IPD.

Goulding, A., and Kerslake, E. (1997) *Training for part-time and temporary workers*, Library Association Publishing.

Hackett, P. (1997) *Introduction to training*, IPD.

Hammond, H. (1999) The Norfolk and Norwich Millennium Library. In McDonald, A., et al. (eds) (1999) *Libraries in the learning community: building strategic partnerships*, University of Sunderland.

Hannaford, C. *Why learning is not all in your head*, Great Ocean Publishers.

Hardingham, A. (1996) *Designing training*, IPD.

Higgins, J. M. (1994) *101 creative problem solving techniques*, New Management Publishing.

Hofstede, G. (1980) *Culture's consequences: international differences in work-related values*, Sage.

Hollands, W. D. (1999) *Teaching the Internet to library staff and users: 10 ready-to-run workshops that work*, Library Association Publishing.

Honey, P. (1992) *The learning log: a way of enhancing learning from experience*, Peter Honey.

Honey, P., and Mumford, A. (1992) *The manual of learning styles*, Peter Honey.

Hopson, N., and Scally, M. (1981) *Lifeskills teaching*, McGraw-Hill.

Hunter, D. (1992) *The Zen of groups*, Gower.

Jensen, E. (1998) *Trainer's Bonanza*, The Brain Store.

Jones, K. (1991) *Icebreakers: a source book of games, exercises and simulations*, Kogan Page.

Kalish, K. (1997) *How to give a terrific presentation*, American Management Association.

Kendall, M. (1990) Training for library work in a multicultural Britain. In Prytherch, R. (ed.) *Handbook of library training practice*, Gower.

Kirby, A. (1992) *Games for trainers 1*, Gower.

Kirby, A. (1992) *Games for trainers 2*, Gower.

Kirby, A. (1994) *Games for trainers 3*, Gower.

Kolb, D. A. (1985) *Experiential learning*, Prentice-Hall.

The Learning Age: A Renaissance for a New Britain (1998), HMSO (Cmnd 3790).

Learning works: widening participation in further education (Chairman: Helena Kennedy, QC) (1997), Further Education Funding Council.

Lewis, D. (1996) Co-training: cost effective staff development, *Brainwaves*.

Library Association (1999) *Presentation skills for library and information professionals*, Library Association.

Maxted, P. (ed.) (1996) *From the Ivory Tower . . . to the street. Putting learning theory into practice. A report on the "Bringing theory to life!" colloquium*, October 29th and 30th 1996, Weetwood Hall, Leeds, Royal Society of Arts.

McDonald, A., et al. (eds) (1999) *Libraries in the learning community: building strategic partnerships*, University of Sunderland.

Morris, B. (1993) *Training and development for women*, Library Association Publishing.

Morrison, K. (1995) Dewey, Habermas and reflective practice, *Curriculum*, **16** (2), 82–130.

National Committee for Enquiry into Higher Education (1997) *Higher education in the learning society*, HMSO (the Dearing Report).

Nelson-Jones, R. (1991) *Lifeskills: a handbook*, Cassell.

O'Connor, J., and Seymour, J. (1994) *Training with NLP: skills for managers, trainers and communicators*, Thorsons.

Open University (1994) *Identifying learning needs and assessing achievement, People and Potential*, Study Unit 2.

Open University (1994) *Planning, monitoring and evaluating learning programmes, People and Potential*, Study Unit 3.

Overdurf, J., and Silverthorn, J. (1995) *Training trances*, Metamorphous Press.

Parkin, M. (1998) *Tales for trainers: using stories and metaphors to facilitate learning*, Kogan Page.

Pressler, C. (1999) STELA – Staff training for electronic access, University College London, *Personnel Training and Education*, **17** (2), 15–17.

Race, P. (1995) *500 tips for teachers*, Kogan Page.

Rickards, T. (1990) *Creativity and problem-solving at work*, Gower.

Rodwell, J. (1994) *Participative training skills*, Gower.

Rose and Goll (1992) *Accelerate your learning*, ALS.

Schon, D. (1983) *The reflective practitioner: how professionals think in action*, Basic Books.

Saunders, M., and Holdaway, K. (1993) *The lone trainer*, Kogan Page.

Siddons, S. (1997) *Delivering training*, IPD.

Smith, A. (1998) *Accelerated learning in practice*, Network Educational Press.

Sugar, S. (1998) *Games that teach*, Jossey-Bass/Pfeiffer.

Thompson, D. (1993) Reflection learning. In *Improving student learning: theory and practice*, Oxford Center for Staff Development.

University of Lincolnshire and Humberside (1999) *Effective learner programme*.

Walton, S. J. (1994) *Cultural diversity in the workplace*, Irwin.

Ward, S. (1999) Information professionals for the next millennium, *Journal of Information Science*, **25** (4), 239–48.

Whetherly, J. (1994) *Management of training and staff development*, Library Association Publishing.

Index

ABOUT THE AUTHOR

Barbara Allan is a senior lecturer in student and management learning for the Hull University Business School, where she is also deputy director of the Centre for Management and Organisational Learning (CMOL). Barbara's background is varied and includes managing workplace and academic libraries and learning resource centers; lecturing in a school of library and information studies; and also working as a freelance trainer, researcher, and author. Barbara has masters' degrees in information science, adult education, and networked collaborative learning (e-learning). In addition, she has a PGCE (Postgraduate Certificate in Education) and is an accredited trainer in neuro-linguistic programming. She became an associate of the Library Association (UK) in 1978 and is currently a member of its successor organization, CILIP. She's also a member of the Institute for Learning and Teaching in Higher Education in the UK.

ABOUT THE NORTH AMERICAN EDITOR

Barbara B. Moran is professor and former dean at the School of Information and Library Science at the University of North Carolina at Chapel Hill. She received an A.B. degree from Mount Holyoke College, an M.Ln. from Emory University, and a Ph.D. in higher education and LIS from the State University of New York at Buffalo, where her dissertation was on the topic of career progression patterns of academic library directors. She teaches primarily in the area of management and has a special interest in human resources management. Dr. Moran is coauthor of the widely used textbook *Management of Libraries and Information Agencies*; the sixth edition of that text was published in September 2002. She is also the author of numerous articles, book chapters, and three other books on various aspects of management and leadership.